A Grand Gathering

Written and Edited by
Sammye Munson

Sammye Munson (signature)

EAKIN PRESS ⬥ Austin, Texas

Dedicated to My Grandchildren

Cover photo: Margaret McLelland holding great-grandson Chris—
the intergenerational link goes on.

FIRST EDITION
Copyright © 2002
By Sammye Munson
Published in the United States of America
By Eakin Press
A Division of Sunbelt Media, Inc.
P.O. Drawer 90159 ⌨ Austin, Texas 78709-0159
email: sales@eakinpress.com
💻 website: www.eakinpress.com 💻
ALL RIGHTS RESERVED.
1   2   3   4   5   6   7   8   9
1-57168-718-1

Library of Congress Cataloging-in-Publication Data

A grand gathering / edited by Sammye Munson.– 1st ed.
   p.   cm.
  ISBN 1-57168-718-1 (alk. paper)
   1. Grandmothers—Texas. 2. Grandparent and child—Texas—
Anecdotes. 3. Grandmothers—Texas—Biography. I. Munson,
Sammye.
HQ759.9.G68 2002
306.874'5'09764–dc21
                                             2002010645

Contents

Gifts and Favors

From Faraway Lands

What Is a Grandparent?

Acknowledgments

Carol Burnett, excerpt from *One More Tune*, Copyright 1986 Kalola Productions. Published by Random House.

Arthur Kornhaber, *Grandparent Power*, Copyright 1994 Dr. Arthur Kornhaber and Sondra Forsyth, Crown Paperbacks.

N. Scott Momaday, excerpt from *The Way to Rainy Mountain*, first published in *The Reporter*, January 26, 1967. Copyright 1969, University of New Mexico Press.

Dan Rather, excerpt from *I Remember*, Copyright 1991, DIR Enterprises, Inc., published by Little Brown and Company.

Eudora Welty, reprinted by permission of the publishers from p. 66 in *One Writer's Beginnings* by Eudora Welty, Cambridge, Mass.: Harvard University Press, Copyright 1983, 1984 Eudora Welty.

Special Thanks and Acknowledgments

Special thanks go to Marci Bahr, curriculum coordinator, St. John's School, Houston, Texas, and her teachers who graciously shared their students' tributes to their grandparents. Also thanks to Cheryl Bickerstaff, teacher, Katy Independent School District, for sharing her students' work.

And a big thank you to all the people who wrote from their hearts the memories they have of their grandparents. Most of the work here has not been published previously but was written for *A Grand Gathering*.

Introduction

Not long ago I heard an octogenerian tell about playing paperdolls under the soundboard of her grandmother's grand piano. She never forgot the feeling of peace and security or the beautiful sounds of Beethoven and Chopin as her grandmother taught music lessons. Another person recalled her grandfather reading the classics to her when she was young, creating the love of literature that has lasted through the years.

Whenever grandparents are mentioned in a gathering, I hear stories, unique memories that people enjoy sharing. They tell anecdotes, both funny and sad, stories that should be shared.

So began my book, *A Grand Gathering*, an anthology of memories about grandmothers and grandfathers. These are true stories about real people. Although many share the theme of the spiritual and emotional bonds between grandparent and grandchild, each is the individual's own memory. How can the simple act of making pickles with a grandmother establish a bond that *exists* in a forty-something woman today?

It does.

Because there are no strings attached, this love does not depend on good behavior or appropriate action as it often does with the parent role. It has been called the purest of all love because it is unconditional and immeasurable. Dr. Arthur Kornhaber of the Foundation for Grandparenting calls this intergenerational bond "the vital connection."

Jean-Paul Sartre once said, "I could make my grandmother go into raptures of joy just by being hungry." (Dr. Arthur Kornhaber 1994).

Grandparents are nurturers. But they are also historians, possessing family memories that go back generations. This creates continuity and a sense of belonging in the child.

With the necessity for many mothers to work outside the home as well as the increase of divorce and broken families, grandparents are more important than ever. They carry the torches of tradition and continuity in a society of change. Grandchildren are beginning their lifespan, while their grandparents are at the opposite end, mellowed with years of experience.

It is estimated that there are over sixty million grandparents in the United States today and with a baby boomer turning fifty every seven seconds, the grandparent population is growing. This might be the most important era in history for grandparent involvement. With E-mail and video cassettes, even faraway grandparents can stay in touch with their grandchildren.

It is the author's hope that readers will find these stories reassuring and will identify with many of them. Perhaps they will learn even more about being a grandparent.

A Grand Gathering is the gift of grandchildren everywhere to you.

—SAMMYE MUNSON

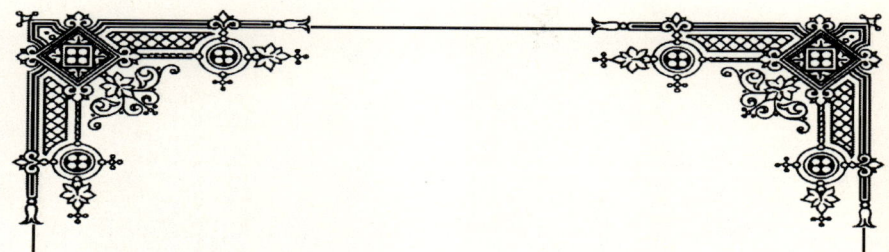

Role Models and Mentors

Grandparents are, by the fact of their age and position in the family, prime targets to be role models and mentors. They have lived a number of years, made mistakes, and achieved successes, and can pass on their wisdom of years to their grandchildren. These grandchildren may be more receptive to their grandparents' advice than to their parents. Consciously or unconsciously, grandchildren may pattern some of their thoughts and ambitions from the examples of their grandparents.

Isabella Bjerring (right) with granddaughter Alison Quoyeser

Letter to Mommy Belle

by Alison Quoyeser

I am writing to you on your ninety-fifth birthday. As you near the age of 100, your birthdays become more precious to me. I have to let you know how much you mean to me.

You became a teacher while you were just a teenager and returned to school to get a master's degree as a widow and mother of two girls. You taught me the value of education and the arts. You have provided a compelling role model for your daughters, granddaughters, and great granddaughters.

How I recall early years. Memories of visiting you in Port Arthur form an almost sacred place in my mind. I remember entering the front screened porch and finding that the begonia plant was threatening to fill the entire place. Inside the house symphonies, sonatas, concertos, and operas sounded between the walls. Running between the rooms we could feel the wood-frame house vibrate on its concrete piers.

Delicious smells emanated from the bright kitchen. You served lunches on the back screened porch—German potato salad, sauerkraut, baked ham, homemade biscuits. You poured lemonade and iced tea with fresh mint leaves we gathered from the garden into those aluminum tumblers that came in different tints of violet, magenta, and turquoise, so that each cousin could have his or her own color.

At night, faces washed and teeth brushed, we would struggle to climb into the tall beds and drift away to the sound of the heavy metal fan thrumming back and forth.

Thanks for being so strong for us and for creating the wonderful place, your home. I wish you many more happy birthdays.

Love, Alison

To the Cotton Gin with Grandpa

by Leslie Munson

I can still see his tall, lean figure dressed in overalls, a straw hat on his head, as he hitched his mules to a wagon loaded with snowy white cotton from his farm. Grandpa worked hard on his hundred acres of good, black farm land in Central Texas, raising a family of six children.

Claus Munson came to Texas from a village in Sweden when he was a boy of fifteen, proud to be in the United States after a difficult economic period in Sweden. He left all schooling behind him and moved in with an older brother and learned to farm cotton. Saving every cent he could, he bought a 100-acre farm, then married another Swedish immigant, Alma Johnson, from Stockholm.

Grandpa was a quiet man, who worked from sunup to sundown in the cotton field. I loved to visit the farm, spend the night, and sleep in the feather bed upstairs in the big farmhouse in the country. And I loved Grandpa—loved to watch him plow the field, feed his cow and chickens.

Each Sunday morning when I was very young, I went to church with my parents. I didn't mind going because I knew I'd see Grandpa. Mother sang in the choir, Dad ushered and took up the collection, and I sat in Grandpa's lap where I promptly fell asleep. Later, I was told that I snored loudly in church, but Grandpa patted me and kept me as quiet as possible.

After church I'd run to Grandpa's car, sit in the back seat, and expect to go home with him and spend the rest of the day. He never disappointed me by telling me I couldn't come.

When I got older, I would put a cotton sack (made by Grandma) over my shoulder and pick cotton. Grandpa taught me to pluck the tops of the bolls just the right way and drop them in

4

Leslie Munson holding the hand of Grandfather Claus Munson
with Wayne Munson, cousin

5

the sack. The cotton was then placed in the wagon. When the wagon was full of cotton, Grandpa picked me up and put me in the center of the cotton. We would head for the gin, me riding like the Little Prince, as he drove the mules to the other side of town. It was my favorite time of the year—late summer—because I could experience the excitement of going to the cotton gin with Grandpa.

The heavy load of cotton cushioned my ride that otherwise would have been mercilessly bumpy. I'd lay on my back and look up at the sky, feeling as if the whole world belonged to me. We passed peach orchards that emitted the sweet smell of ripening fruit.

At the gin I climbed down from the wagon and stayed close to Grandpa. The machinery rattled so loudly that we had to yell to be heard. I watched the tube suck up the cotton into a machine that separated seeds from fiber. I held Grandpa's calloused hand tightly as the machinery clanged and shook. I knew I was safe with him nearby. We stayed until all the cotton had been ingested in the machine, weighed, and baled. At that time Grandpa might smile widely, or frown, depending on the payment he received for six months of hard work.

After he was paid, we climbed back into the wagon with me sitting beside him and drove to the farm. Grandma always prepared a good country dinner (the noon meal was called dinner then). We'd have fried chicken, corn, tomatoes, green beans—all from the farm. And for dessert she made *ost kaka*, the Swedish custard similar to cheesecake. After the exciting morning at the gin and the big meal, I fell asleep. When I awoke, I watched the clock until 4:00 P.M. when I took Grandpa his coffee in the field. No matter how hot it was, he had to have his 4:00 o'clock coffee with cookies or something sweet to eat.

Grandpa's first language was Swedish, and the language he was most comfortable speaking. Yet he always spoke English to me. He was so happy to be in America and always felt proud his children and grandchildren were Americans and spoke English well.

6

Quilt of Love
by Mary Belle Patterson

She was barely five feet tall and had the bluest eyes I've ever seen. She had no sense of humor, was a strict disciplinarian, and lived by the Ten Commandments. We were sometimes frightened by her but still loved her dearly. She was my grandmother, and we were my father, mother, and seven-year-old me.

We went to live with her when the Great Depression caused us to lose our income and our home. All we had was a Packard touring car. Others in Grandmother's family suffered the same fate. So there she was, a widow with two teenagers of her own, my family, my uncle's family, an unmarried uncle, all living in the house she owned on the outskirts of town.

Grandmother told all the aunts what to do in the kitchen. She told the uncles what to do in the yard to keep everything looking nice. Everyone had a job to do. She said that idleness was the devil's workshop.

Grandmother married a young neighbor when she was nineteen, and they began farming on adjacent land. Eventually, they had ten children. When she was forty-five, her husband died of pneumonia. She had five children under seventeen to raise and nothing else but a farm. Three older boys enlisted in the marines during World War I. When they returned, they learned their father was dead. One young man was disabled and was sent to a veterans' hospital. Another son had been gassed and remained in ill health for the rest of his short life. Still, Grandmother worked hard and kept her faith in God.

A few years later, one of her younger sons didn't want to stay on the farm and ran away from home with the intent of joining the navy. It was a heart-stopping experience when two railroad detectives came to her door to tell her that her son and his friend had been killed while sleeping on the railroad tracks. She should have

Grandmother Molly Belle Page
with granddaughter Mary Belle Patterson

been extremely depressed, but she rose to the occasion with spirit and faith.

Our little grandmother attended church every Sunday. On Tuesday she went to the Missionary Society meeting and on Wednesday night to prayer meeting.

My cousins and I liked to go to Sunday church with her because we received so much attention. If there was a visiting preacher, he came to our house for Sunday dinner. Platters of fried chicken, fresh green beans, mashed potatoes, and hot steaming peach cobbler awaited him and us. There were plenty of drumsticks and wings for us, the children, who ate at a second table.

The ladies of the Missionary Society came often to help with the quilting. A quilt-top piece sewn by hand from scraps of material with batting on a backing was placed in a frame and lowered from the ceiling in the parlor. Thimbles and needles flew as the ladies gathered around it, quilting intricate patterns on the fabric.

Franklin D. Roosevelt was elected that year. Grandmother was sure that better times were coming. She gathered us all each evening in the parlor. We said a short prayer to thank God for His blessings. Then my uncles would get out their guitars and a violin. We sang and laughed and had the best time.

Finally, my dad got a job in a nearby town. We packed our car and left Grandmother's house. How I hated to leave my cousins, aunts, and uncles. But most of all, I hated to leave Grandmother. I was her namesake and I'll always remember the things she taught me. She was called Molly Belle, and I am Mary Belle.

Because of her I'll always have faith in myself and in the future. That faith is woven into Grandmother's quilt that I still keep on my bed.

The Secret of the Stones

by Tess Thomas

On a lazy Sunday afternoon in 1939, when I was seven years old, Grandpa James Doty Richman and I traipsed across a meadow of buttercups and climbed Cemetery Hill, overlooking the southern sawmill town we called home. Pine trees over a hundred feet tall stood as sentinels over the graves. A warm breeze smelled of honeysuckle while a mockingbird chattered angrily.

Grandpa settled his lanky frame on a nearby log and pulled his pipe and can of Prince Albert tobacco from his pocket. He struck a long kitchen match along the thigh of his trousers and lit the pipe bowl. Then he watched as I scurried about, searching beneath the bushes for stones I'd hidden the previous visit. Stones the size of hen eggs, some larger, some smaller. Some sparkling with veins of silver that Grandpa brought back from Colorado, volcanic rock from New Mexico and just ordinary brown stones from the woods.

While piling the stones atop the graves, I asked, "Why do we do this, Grandpa? I know you said it shows respect, but why?"

He took a deep breath and let out a long sigh. "Well, I've heard several versions, but the one that sounds the most logical is that in Biblical days wild animals sometimes dug up freshly buried bodies. For protection, people began covering the graves with stones. In time, the stones got scattered or disappeared. So each visitor to a grave site, out of respect, added one new stone. As the pile of stones grew, it showed that the dead person had many friends in life."

"But wild animals don't dig up these graves."

"No, but it's still a way of showing love and respect."

By the time Grandpa finished his explanation, I had constructed neat piles of stones on all the graves. I sat quietly beside him on the fallen tree trunk. Then it occurred to me that this

10

Grandpa James Doty with grandchildren
Tess Thomas and Harold Bolton

seemed like a lot of needless work. "Grandpa, why don't we leave the stones in place?"

His face scrunched into a frown and he cocked his head to one side. Thinking I'd made him angry, I bent my head in shame and pushed a clump of violets with my toe.

"Come, sit beside me, girl. I reckon if you're old enough to ask, it's time you knew the truth. Placing stones on graves is a Jewish tradition. If we leave them there, people will know that we're Jewish. Then life wouldn't be as comfortable for us as it is now."

I tried to absorb this strange revelation. If Grandpa was Jewish, didn't that mean that I was, too?

"Don't mention this to anyone, Child. Someday people's attitudes will change. Prejudice will disappear. But until that time, keep this secret."

And so, we continued to live the lie. In the following months, Grandpa became preoccupied with news accounts of a man named Hitler whose goose-stepping army was marching across Poland, destroying everything in its path. This was the only time I ever saw tears on Grandpa's face. He still had family living in Poland.

Grandpa died in April the following year before the United States entered World War II. He died without knowing what happened to his relatives in Poland. He never knew about the Nazi concentration camps or the gas chambers into which many Jewish families were herded like cattle. He never saw pictures of bodies stacked like firewood in ovens. But I know. I've heard stories of survivors that I will never forget.

And never, ever again, will I hide stones placed on my family's graves.

Grandpa Harrison, He Cast a Mighty Long Shadow

by Anna Pearl Barrett

Anna Pearl Barrett

Harrison Barrett, our grandpa, triumphed over slavery, segregation, and hard times. He became a businessman and Texas land baron, who had big dreams and a vision of what he wanted for himself and his family. Uncle Porter always told us, "Pa was a big man, he done big things, dreamt big dreams, and made 'em come true. He casted a mighty long shadow."

Sitting on the front porch on warm summer evenings, Uncle Porter would tell us about Grandpa, who was born a slave in Texas about 1851. He was a handsome man, tall and broad-shouldered with brown eyes and light brown skin and a shock of reddish-brown curls. He bought land when slaves and ex-slaves didn't own the right to themselves, let alone land. Freedmen and freedwomen often lived on credit and sweat, in shacks and shanties. Not our grandpa.

"When Pa was a young slave," Uncle Porter said, "he'd stand in them cotton fields in the sizzling sun, lean on his hoe and think, 'The Lord's got to make a way. I ain't living my life like this.' And he didn't."

Grandpa Harrison became the master's right-hand man, which allowed him to leave the scorching sun and backbreaking work behind. He took care of plantation business, traveling throughout the South and Southwest. He went as far as Virginia, bringing a bride, Grandma Anne Jones, back to Texas.

"When the news 'bout freedom got to Texas two-and-a-half years after them 'Mancipation laws got signed, it was June 19, 1865," Uncle Porter told us. "Pa saved his money, burying it in a safe place. He worked hard, cutting and selling wood, catching, taming, and selling wild horses, and squirreled away his money.

"In 1867 Pa and Ma got married, him sixteen and her thirteen. Just children. Ma lived in the 'big house' doing fancy sewing for ladies, and they paid her. She and Pa always knew they'd get married, and they did it right. Ma wouldn't hear of no 'taking up' or broom jumping. Ma wanted a proper wedding and she got it. White frilly dress, veil, the works. Folks far and near still talk about her 'highfalutin' Virginia ways.

"Hard times hit the South after the war. The ex-masters had little money for themselves, none for ex-slaves. Freedom threw most into a tizzy," Uncle Porter said. "Ain't no schools that get you ready for freedom."

Uncle Porter told us about Juneteenth. "Old General Gordon Granger brought the freedom news to Galveston on June 19, 1865. They called it Juneteenth. What a commotion broke out when the news hit: praying, singing, dancing. There was no celebrating for Pa. He'd saved enough money to start buying land. He cut wood and built his own house. Although ex-slaves could not own land, he struck a deal with a white landowner and by 1866 owned over forty acres.

"Pretty soon Pa lit out to find his sold-off family," Uncle Porter said. "He never found his sister Leatha but he found Aunt Betty, Uncle Tobe, Uncle Frank, and their families."

By 1870 Grandpa Harrison had acquired more than 200 acres near downtown Houston. He donated land to help build Barrett's School and Shiloh Baptist Church, one of the oldest black churches in the state. The community was called Barretts Settlement until the mid 1940s when the United States government opened a post office and the area became Barrett's Station. Today, the Texas official highway map and Texas Almanac list the community simply as Barrett after our Grandpa Harrison Barrett.

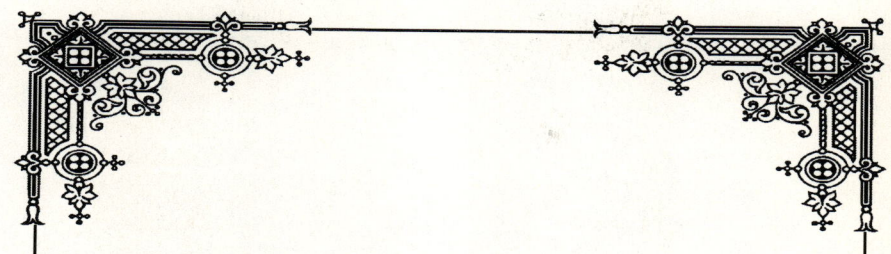

Grandparents As Parents

For generations grandparents have been caregivers for their grandchildren. They have assumed this role part-time or full time, temporarily or permanently. When death, divorce, or other tragedy occurs, grandparents often take the reins. They console, comfort, and even become surrogate parents.

Today with so many working mothers, grandparents may keep children after school or when they're ill, take them to music, dance, or athletic events. They fill a need for their children and grandchildren.

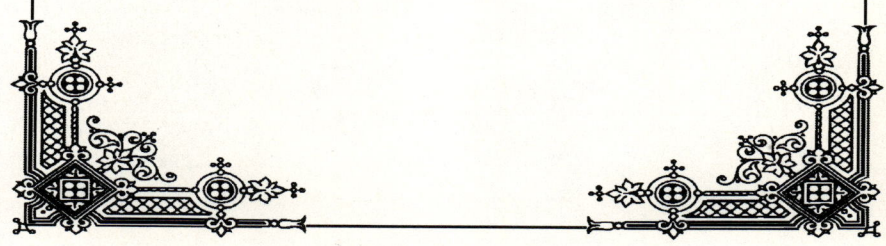

Guadalupe Quintanilla and
Grandmother "Nana" in Mexico

Nana, Mi Abuela

by Guadalupe Quintanilla

My grandmother, Nana, used to tell me that I was her "special gift." Later, I learned that my parents, who lived in the same town, divorced when I was born. My mother moved to another city and took me with her.

When my father realized my mother was abusing me, he took me to his parent's home and delivered me into Nana's arms. This is how I became Nana's whole world. She made me feel as though her life revolved around me. Looking back, I realize how skillful she was to manage her responsibilities, her time, and me.

Nana was a pretty woman who looked almost fragile but who was very strong. She had green eyes that smiled all the time. She sang all kinds of songs and laughed heartily at the slightest provocation. I never heard her complain about aches, pains, or problems.

Nana's long hair was black and silver. One of my delights, as a child, was to sit by her side and watch her braid her hair. She folded the braid on top of her head and secured it with hairpins. As she fixed my hair the same way, I felt beautiful and loved. Later, she taught me how to braid my hair as she did.

My grandfather, Tats I called him, was quite an entrepreneur. He had different businesses in Mexico but also had a job with the government and was gone most of the time.

Nana managed a grocery store, bicycle shop, popsicle factory, bakery, her household, and me.

Nana got up early each morning to supervise the baking of bread that we sold in the store.

When the aroma of freshly baked bread awakened me at 6:00 A.M., breakfast was ready, and I heard Nana and the baker carrying trays of bread to the front of the store. In our two-story home, we lived upstairs, and the store and bakery were downstairs.

Part of the morning ritual was teaching me to do household

17

chores. Nana taught by example. She had me do a task as many times as necessary to get it right. It was important to complete a chore as well as I could.

Nana always told me not to walk backwards, as a child likes to do sometimes. One afternoon I stayed behind as Nana rushed to wait on a customer at the bakery. I was walking backwards, tripped, and fell into a tub full of eggs. As the crackling of the eggs intensified, so did my fears. What would I tell Nana?

Suddenly, I looked up and saw my grandmother's horrified face looking anxiously at me. She was afraid I was hurt. She pulled me from the sea of broken eggs and hugged me, eggs and all. I felt her tears, tears of relief, on her cheeks. I learned then that tears can come from joy as well as from sorrow.

Nana taught herself to read and write. And she taught me the joy of learning. We often sat side by side and read together. I remember those books even now—stories of adventure, fairies, and magic. Nana would encourage me to read to the most interesting part of the story. Then she would stop me, and I would have to wait until the next day to see how it ended. When the next day came, I ran around her as she did the chores, chanting, "Let's read now, Nana, please."

I remember her laughter as we both stumbled, trying to pronounce a difficult word. She made a game of finding words in the dictionary and using them in sentences.

Once she said, "Education is the only thing that I can leave you, and the only one that you will never use up or forget."

I have never forgotten those words. They gave me intellectual curiosity and the determination to be all that I can be.

One of my most persistent questions was, "Nana, why am I shorter than everyone else?"

"Because many fine things come in very small packages," she would reply with a smile and a grandmother's caring.

Hardly a day passes that I do not feel Nana's presence in my life. She guided me to become a happy, strong, confident woman. Because of her example, I learned to appreciate the most important things in life: health, happiness, love, and time to enjoy them all.

Ma and Pa Buckles

by Estelle Moore-Walker

Ma and Pa Buckles (John and Estelle Buckles) were my grandparents, my mother's parents. They lived in Fayette, Mississippi, a small town located in the central part of the state (population 2,500). My grandparents contributed most to my upbringing.

Living in rural Mississippi, neither could drive and never owned a car. Yet they understood the necessity of a quality education and quality extra-curricular activities. Education was an absolute priority. My grandparents, with their meager farmer's income, managed to pay a neighbor to take me to weekly piano lessons, to club meetings, and to school dances. When the band performed, when I played in a recital or participated in any school function, my grandparents were always there.

In the 1960s, when my area of Mississippi began integrating schools, my grandparents insisted that I attend the integrated school. Looking back at those turbulent times, I am amazed at the courage of that decision, the strength they instilled in me to endure hostility, and the foresight to realize what true value education is. I hope that in my present career as a high school teacher that I am able to instill in my pupils the same determination and knowledge.

Ma was a strong, determined, and caring grandmother. She prepared our scrumptious meals, washed our dirty laundry, cleaned our home, and gave much advice. She sat up with me when I was ill, coaxing me to drink herb tea. She would listen patiently as I recited endless notes for upcoming tests and was the first person who told me I could be successful at whatever I chose to do. Ma was the first person to explain the concept of God, church, and the whole business of honesty, integrity, and pride.

Pa was a warm, loving, patient, and handsome grandfather. He was the quiet listener, rarely judgmental. Pa got up early each day and did the chores on our small farm. On cold mornings, Pa would precede my going to the highway where the bus stop was. He would pile brush and sticks to build a fire so I would keep warm waiting for the school bus.

I remember one dark, stormy afternoon in my junior year in high school. I missed the bus home but later got a ride with a friend. I arrived home two hours after my scheduled drop-off. As the car approached the entrance to our winding road, I saw Pa standing patiently with my umbrella and raincoat. I was brought to tears at the sight of him waiting, not knowing what hour I would arrive. Our home was a quarter of a mile from the highway. But Ma and Pa would wait for the bus with my rain gear if the weather changed for the worse during the day.

I also remember Pa walking into the woods with me to pick out a Christmas tree. He was patient as I surveyed every tree in sight and finally chose the perfect tree. He'd then cut it down with his axe and drag it home.

Ma and Pa were present in every phase of my life. They were there during my earliest years, my school functions, my illnesses, junior high and high school, and finally graduation. They encouraged me during my college years and were proud when I received my college diploma. And when I decided to marry, Ma paid for my wedding gown, and Pa gave me away. How fortunate I was to have such a nurturing environment and the opportunities to fulfill my ambition to become a teacher.

Bird Song

by Pam Zollman

My sister and I lived with my grandparents, who adopted us when I was six. I always felt as if they were my real parents. We used to joke about the generational gap and how there wasn't one in our family. My grandmother demanded respect as the disciplinarian. But Papa spoiled me rotten, giving me whatever I wanted.

One thing he couldn't give me, though, was the ability to whistle. Papa tried to teach me, but somehow I could never get my tongue, teeth, and lips in the right position. My sister Colleen learned quickly, joining Papa in whistling a variety of songs and bird calls. I sounded like a teapot coming to a full boil.

Papa loved to sit on the front porch and imitate the mockingbirds in the mimosa tree. No matter how complicated the mockingbird's song, Papa could copy it. It confused the mockingbirds, making them swoop around the yard looking for the other bird.

"Carl," my grandmother would say, "are you teasing those birds again?"

"They don't mind." he'd reply. "It's a game we play."

Papa died suddenly of a heart attack when I was twenty and he was eighty. My grandmother was too overcome with grief to make the funeral arrangements. That became my job. I didn't have time to cry as I picked out the casket and clothes he would wear.

The first night after Papa died. I couldn't sleep, tossing and turning. All four windows in the room were open to catch the breeze. About midnight a bird began singing. A solitary mockingbird sat outside my window in the mimosa tree singing complicated bird tunes.

For some reason this upset me. Whoever heard of birds singing in the middle of the night? I hid my head under the pillow. I closed the windows. I opened the windows and yelled at the bird.

21

I threw my brush at it, but nothing stopped the mockingbird. At dawn it became quiet and flew away.

"Did you hear that stupid bird?" I asked my grandmother that morning.

"Yes, I listened to it all night." She smiled, the first time since Papa died. "Didn't you like the bird song?"

"No. Stupid bird has no respect for the dead."

"It reminded me of Carl," my grandmother said.

"Papa?" I thought.

The next night as I lay in bed, about midnight I saw a solitary mockingbird in the mimosa tree and heard it sing until dawn. I still couldn't cry but finally I thought of Papa's teasing whistle and fell asleep.

The third night I looked forward to the mockingbird's song. It began about midnight, and I fell asleep listening to it.

The next day was the funeral and a hard day for all of us. After the relatives left that night, I collapsed into bed, feeling sad and lonely. I looked forward to the mockingbird's song at midnight. Midnight came, but the mockingbird did not. I stayed awake until dawn, waiting for the familiar song. When the sun rose. I arose, too, eager for the quiet night to end. I looked out at the mimosa tree and began to cry, shedding the tears trapped inside me. I finally could express my grief.

Now, every time I hear a mockingbird's song, I think of Papa.

Love Comes in Many Ways
by Betty Diener

My father was in the navy when I was young and since my mother was not the adventurous type, we lived with her parents while he was at sea. Eventually, my parents separated and the only father figure I ever knew was Grandfather Yetter. I was his first grandchild and since we lived with him and Grandmother, I was a bit spoiled.

I could usually count on Grandfather to take my side if Mother and I differed. This happened often at mealtime since I disliked vegetables. Yet his patience was not endless, and he could get upset with me. The summers were as warm in 1920 in Philadelphia as they are now in Houston. Wool rugs were taken up and cleaned before storing in the attic for summer. We hung them on the clothes line in the back yard and beat them with a wire beater to get rid of the dust.

My grandfather had cleaned the rug and rolled it up to take back to the house. He carried it behind him with his hands rolled under the rug. I picked up the wire beater to give the rug a few more swats, but I swatted his hands instead. He let out a yell of pain and dropped the rug. I ran into the house, up the stairs, and crawled under the bed to avoid his reprimand. I stayed there for a long time until he calmed down. I never received the punishment I deserved. Grandfather was my strongest supporter and told me I could do anything I wanted to do. He was always there to encourage me and praise my efforts.

Grandfather had a workshop in his cellar and made many of my toys. I wanted a doll house, and he decided to build one for me. I had to stay away from the cellar since it was my Christmas present. The doll house became quite large and did not fit into my bedroom. It had to be put into a room in the attic where I enjoyed many happy hours playing with it.

Grandfather Frank Yetter and
granddaughter Betty Steward Diener

Of course, I needed furniture, so Grandfather began making it. The living room had a fireplace with electric lights (Christmas lights) so the hearth would appear real. Everyone marveled at the house. Grandfather made a brass door opener so the door would actually shut with a latch he contrived.

The windows slid up and down, and the stairway had a walnut handrail with small spindles to support it. The two-story house had a roof with shingles cut to look authentic. Each room in the house had a small light in the ceiling with a light fixture he made. He also made doll furniture for the house. It was quite an occasion for cousins and friends to visit and view my doll house. I was the envy of all of them.

One Christmas Grandfather made me a high chair for my dolls. I loved it and played with it for years. When my own daughter was old enough, he salvaged it from the attic, repainted it, and sent it to her for Cbristmas.

24

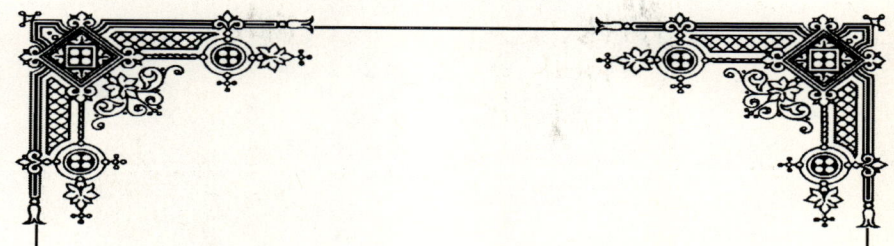

Celebrities and Grandparents

No matter how famous or well known a person becomes, he or she never forgets those early memories, especially of grandparents. The love given and the experiences shared remain an indelible part of the grandchild's life.

Dan Rather recalls a poignant experience with his grandmother in "Of Dream Books and Bibles." Laura Bush, first lady of the United States, can never forget a "Grandmother Who Could Do Anything." Carol Burnett also shares an experience with Nanny, her grandmother.

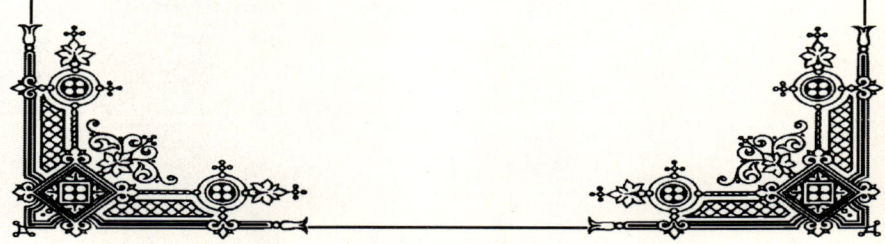

Dan Rather

Of Dream Books and Bibles

(Excerpt from *I Remember*)

by Dan Rather

I doubt that Grandma Page went beyond the sixth grade and hers was not a home filled with books. Sitting by her coal lamp, she read aloud to Mother from her precious copy of the Sears Roebuck Catalog about garden seeds and other items of home interest. Mother was the youngest and considered the brightest. Eventually, she would finish high school, the only one to have done so to that point.

By the time I came along, not much had changed except the edition of the catalog. Grandmother Page read me page after page. I don't remember that she ever ordered anything. The Sears Catalog was her dream book. Its content wasn't about garden seeds. It was about her dreams.

I also believe she thought that the act of reading was important for deepening a child's interests. Grandma all but revered reading.

"Come, Danny, I'll read to you," she would say. That was enough to make me come running. It meant story time and story time most often was Bible time. The Bible was literally an open book for all the Rathers.

Grandma Page was well aware of my favorite Bible stories and catered to my taste for the great deeds it recorded, especially those of Joshua at the Battle of Jericho. . . . Bible offerings were meant less to serve the cause of piety than our need for entertainment. Joshua was my Sylvester Stallone. Grandma's house had no electricity and no radio. We had to reach out for simple forms of fun in Bloomington, Texas.

Grandmother Could Do Anything

by Laura Bush

My maternal grandmother, Jessie Laura Hawkins, was born in Waco, Texas, in 1898. She moved to El Paso with her husband, my grandfather and their child (my mother) in 1927. They settled in the foothills of the upper Rio Grande Valley where they built a tourist court and store.

My father told me that when my mother brought him home to meet her parents, my grandmother was laying brick when they arrived. Dad always thought he had married into a family whose women could do anything.

My grandmother could make anything. When I was a child, she hand-stitched dresses for me and mailed them to Midland, Texas, where Mom, Dad, and I lived. Each package she mailed contained not only a beautiful dress for me, but also dresses for my dolls, which she made from the left-over scraps of material. She also hand-crafted furniture for my dolls. One of the prettiest pieces was a miniature couch sewn with gold braid. I received all her wonderful creations with great joy and appreciation for her love. I considered myself truly blessed to have such a devoted and talented grandmother.

Underneath her thimble was a green thumb. Long before it was in style, my grandmother was interested in native plants, and her flower beds and rock gardens were filled with lantanas, yuccas, ocotillos, and cacti.

My grandmother's life overflowed with beauty, and she was always committed to her family. She loved to laugh—she loved life—and I was lucky to inherit that.

Laura Bush, grandmother Jessie Hawkins, and mother Jenna Welch

I Remember Nanny

Introduction by Sammye Munson
Excerpt from Carol Burnett's autobiography,
One More Time

Carol Burnett lived with her grandmother, "Nanny," as a small child when her parents separated and her mother left to pursue a career. Carol speaks of the salty, independent grandmother in loving tones in her autobiography, *One More Time*. They were poor and lived in run-down houses or apartments. But the love they shared was profound, especially to a little girl whose parents were gone. Carol and Nanny loved going to movies together even though they were bargain matinees.

"Nanny and I hardly ever went to a first-run movie because it cost too much, but I loved hanging around Grauman's Chinese Theater, where all the movie stars put their hands and feet in wet cement and signed their names. People came from all over the world to stand in the footprints and see how big or little their idol's feet were. And all Nanny and I had to do was walk a few blocks, and there we were.

"Nanny had a habit of watching me leave for school when I was little until the very last possible moment. We had a routine. I'd kiss her good-bye in 102, and then I'd open the door and leave. When I had crossed the lobby and opened that door, I'd turn around, and there she'd be, waving, about seven feet away. I'd wave back, blow her a kiss, and go through the lobby door. I'd look back, and she'd blow one back at me. Then, when I got outside to the sidewalk, I'd look back again, and there she was, at the lobby door: kiss, kiss, blow, blow, wave, wave. Halfway down Wilcox, on the way to Hollywood Boulevard, I'd turn around again, and I'd see her little head and her hand held up, around the corner of the

30

building ... as if I were going off to war. We kept it up until we couldn't see each other anymore."

Carol still remembers that special love that a grandmother gave her.

Eudora Welty

Eudora's Grandfather

Introduction by Sammye Munson
Story by Eudora Welty from her autobiography,
One's Writer's Beginnings

Eudora Welty visited her paternal grandparents during summers, traveling to southern Ohio near the small town of Logan. She describes the house as narrow-porched, two-story, painted white in the Pennsylvania Germany country. Her experiences there influenced her life, her writing.

"I ran to the barn where all you touched was warm. Grandpa's barn was bigger than his house. There was an old buggy being used for hens to nest in, standing in the shadows of the barn. The shiny black buggy next to it, with fringe on top, was the one in which Grandpa drove us to church. He allowed me to stand between his knees and hold the reins, even though I could not see over the horse's tail to where we were going. But standing up on the back seat, I could see, squinting through the peephole window at the back, where the narrow wheels on a rainy Sunday sliced the road to chocolate ribbons. I got to hear Grandpa's voice on Sunday more than any other day, because he sang in the choir; indeed, Grandpa led the choir.

"I think now, in looking back on these summer trips—this one and a number later, made by car or train—that another element must have been influencing my mind. The trips were wholes unto themselves. They were stories. Not only in form, but in their taking on direction, movement, development, change. They changed something in my life: each trip made its particular revelation, though I could not have found words for it. But with the passage of time, I could look back on them and see them bringing me news, discoveries, premonitions, promises. I still can; they still do."

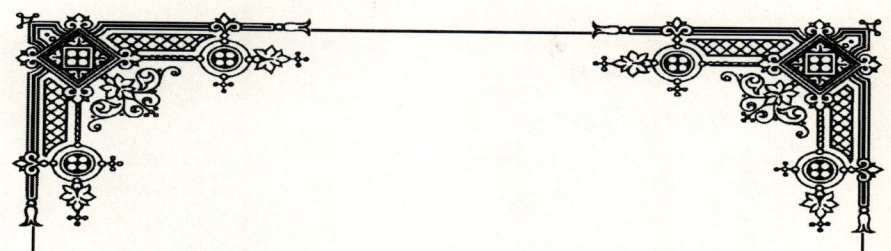

Fun and Laughter

Each of us has a personal memory of a grandparent. Perhaps it was the day that Grandmother demonstrated how to roll out sticky cookie dough, cut it carefully with a metal form, then watch with a smile on her face as the grandchild ate the scrapings from the bowl.

It may have been the day Granddad taught his grandchild how to bait a hook with a squirmy worm or let his grandchild blow on his treasured clarinet.

Travel with a grandparent evokes special memories as does the simple chore of making pickles together. The stories that follow are ones that grandchildren remember with joy in their hearts.

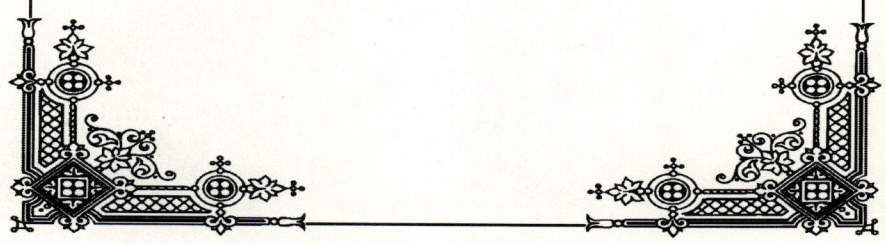

Matthias L. Meyer with granddaughters
Joan Nixon (standing) and her sister Pat

36

That Extra-Special Love

by Joan Nixon

Until I was twelve, my mother, father, two little sisters, and I lived in a duplex in Los Angeles with my mother's parents. A playroom was added to the house and tied the two sides of the duplex together. My parents and grandparents had their own home and privacy; yet they could visit back and forth and share meals together.

The best part for me and my sisters was having my grandparents close and spending time with them. Nanny, my grandmother, spent hours playing card games and Chinese checkers with us, and Pa, my retired grandfather, read countless books to us.

My father had bought us a large wooden pull-wagon which held two children, and on the back was a step for a third child to stand on, with posts on each side to hold. Nearly every afternoon Pa would put Marilyn, Pat, and me in the wagon for a ride. Being the eldest, I usually won the privilege of standing on the step. Then, with seemingly endless energy, Pa would pull us for blocks.

Each Christmas Eve we had a special wagon ride to church to see the manger scene. I loved to see the manger filled with straw, experience the silence of the church, and see the soft light that cast purple shadows.

And I loved thinking of what was happening at that moment. Santa Claus, who started his rounds early, would be arriving at our house. We always returned too late to see him, but maybe this time we'd be lucky.

Unfortunately, this never happened. When we arrived home, Mother would rush in saying, "You just missed Santa Claus. He brought your presents and left no more than two minutes ago."

Love in a Jar

by Anita Higman

My grandmother always found time to make her homemade watermelon pickles. This unique delicacy slid into my mouth with a stinging, sweet sensation. The taste hinted of melon, yet took on a life of its own. Made from half-eaten leftover melon, the pickles were dressed in pink, white, and green pastels as if they had been invited to some great pickling ball. Yes, Grandma loved to make that watermelon treat. I knew it was on her list of joys.

And I was on that list of joys, as well.

She always found time for me, too. Especially games. Grandma and I must have played a million rounds of dominoes and checkers. I don't think I ever cared who won. It was just pure contentment to be near her.

Besides the games, Grandma enjoyed sneaking in bits of life stuff, too. She gave me my first sip of coffee, told me some of the mysteries of human beings, and allowed me to try on her collection of glorious hats.

And holidays and birthdays! My goodness! Grandma let you know you had celebrated, big time. Even ordinary Sunday evenings sparkled with her magic. We always looked forward to sitting on her lawn glider in the cool of the evening to see the stars. We gobbled mounds of cherry cobbler and watched fireflies dance around us as we talked.

As I look back upon the past, pleasant memories abound. Grandma greeted me with a smile and touched my face. I remember her soft stole when she dressed up and her heavenly scent of delicate powder. My finest memory is the unmistakable feeling that she cherished me. If she were alive today, I'd tell her how dear she still is to me and how much she enriched my life. I didn't know how to express this as a young child and didn't realize how precious time and love were.

Grandma put a lot of effort and love into those jars of watermelon pickles. Just as she gave me immeasurable time and unconditional love.

Anita Breitling Higman and brother Jerry Breitling

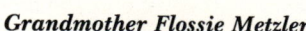

Grandmother Flossie Metzler

39

Paperdolls Under the Piano

by Carolyn Harrell Kilgore

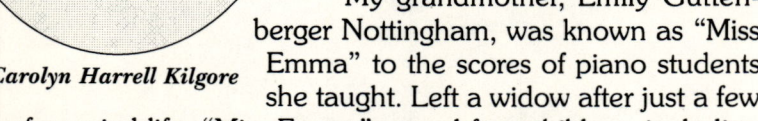

Carolyn Harrell Kilgore

The two-story clapboard house in which I was born in Macon, Georgia, was on a pleasant, elm-shaded street within walking distance of Wesleyan College and Conservatory of Music. At almost any time of day or night, a cacophony of musical sounds escaped from the student practice rooms. My great-grandfather, Phillip Gerhart Guttenberg, was the respected and beloved professor of music at the college for forty years.

My grandmother, Emily Guttenberger Nottingham, was known as "Miss Emma" to the scores of piano students she taught. Left a widow after just a few years of married life, "Miss Emma" reared four children, including my mother, in the house her father, Phillip, willed to her. Although all his children received music educations, my grandmother was able to support her children by teaching lessons on Phillip's Steinway Grand piano.

The highly polished mahogany Steinway piano had been moved from the conservatory after my grandfather's death to the living room at home. I was about three years old when I began to notice the activity around me. I was nine years old when Grandmother died in 1920. It was during those years that she and I became constant companions.

My favorite spot for setting up a paperdoll house was under the sounding board of the piano on the floor while Grandmother practiced. I learned that if I played quietly and if Grandmother was by herself, I was welcome to stay and play with my paperdolls. And listen to her music.

My older sister, Emily, at twelve, was showing a decided musical ability. I earned the privilege of playing under the piano while Emily had her lessons with Grandmother by being very still and quiet.

Taking care of my baby brother and managing the household consumed much of my mother's daytime hours. When I awakened each morning, instead of going to Mother for help, I learned to listen for the soft sounds of Grandmother's playing. I'd tumble from bed, pad barefoot to the living room, and stand quietly by Grandmother who was seated at the piano.

When she noticed me, she'd say, "Come, let's get dressed."

Teeth brushed, bathroom chores attended to, and dressed, we'd return to the living room and the piano. Grandmother began playing scales and simple tunes. I opened up my box of paperdolls and set up the doll house under the shining baby grand piano.

Sounds of the awakening household blended with the musical sounds from the piano. I loved those pre-breakfast concerts at Grandmother's feet. When her health began to decline, she continued teaching piano lessons to many neighborhood children by lying on a small couch by the piano.

I remember once I was swinging slowly on the porch swing outside the window where Grandmother reclined by the piano. My sister, Emily, was playing "Moonlight Sonata" under my grandmother's direction. I can still hear the sound and see the image of the two of them.

This was the last memory I have of Miss Emma, my grandmother. She died a short time later in 1920 when I was nine. She left me a priceless legacy: love of music and love of life that continues to live through my children, grandchildren and sixteen great grandchildren.

41

Moms and the Missing Dime

by Baker Akin

Moms, as I called my grandmother, was only thirty-seven years old when I was born. Since my mother was only eighteen, she was more than happy to share me with Moms.

Moms grew up poor and knew the value of a dime and even a penny. She was the thriftiest one in the family and the one other family members called on for a loan when they were broke. She always had cash stashed away for an emergency.

Moms loved to travel but did it by cutting corners and keeping track of every dime she spent, literally. She and my grandfather took my mother and uncle on long car trips when they were young, often camping out. They continued traveling until he could no longer drive. Yet Moms still had that itching foot and wanted to keep traveling. She called on me, a teenager and oldest grandchild, to drive her on these marathon car trips. We got along well, and I was delighted to have the adventure of seeing new places and having new experiences. But traveling with Moms was both a pleasure and a challenge.

She gave me money each morning to take care of the food, gas, and other expenses. She kept a written record of how much we spent each day and how we spent it. One night we were getting ready for bed in a typical tourist court of the 1940s. She suddenly announced that she could not account for ten cents. We thought and thought but could not remember where that dime went. Finally, in irritation, I told her I had bought a ten-cent piece of ice. She wasn't completely convinced, but at least we could go to sleep that night.

The next morning she woke early and said loudly, "Now I remember. I spent that dime at the grocery store. You didn't buy ice."

At last she had her peace. I understood her need to economize although she was trying at times. Still, she and I spent many

42

happy summers traveling when I was a teenager. I also spent much time in her home when I needed to escape the turmoil of a big family. With her I could be myself and receive undivided attention.

She influenced my life in many ways. I certainly learned the value of money from Moms. This lesson in life helped me succeed in the business world as an adult.

And come summer, when the weather is right, I have to get in the car, take off and travel across the country, see new places, have new experiences. Moms remains with me in spirit.

Baker Akin

Dr. F. C. Bennett,
grandfather

Clayton Kellogg,
granddaughter

44

"Doc," My Grandfather

by Clayton Kellogg

My maternal grandfather was very special to me. We lived in the same town, always shared the same birthdays and holidays. Indeed, we lived in the same house (his) for a few years. I was his first grandchild.

My earliest memory of him is waiting for him to come home from his office late in the afternoon. He was a doctor (eyes, ears, nose and throat) with an office on the fifth floor of a downtown bank. As you walked in the lobby, the first thing you saw was a cigar and newstand. Nickel packages of gum drops, mints, and chewing gum were sold. Flat tin boxes holding fifty cigarettes and all sorts of chewing tobacco were for sale as well as were a few expensive boxes of chocolates that were bought at the last minute for forgotten anniversaries or birthdays.

The spotless lobby held newly polished cuspidors and tall brass ash receptacles lined with layers of clean, white sand. As I passed by the cuspidors, I always took a peek inside but was jerked away rapidly by an adult. Doc never failed to bring me a package of mints or gumdrops at the end of the day, which he gave me as he left his Ford (called Henry by my grandmother). My mother begged him not to give me candy right before supper, but he did anyway.

On Sunday mornings Doc went to the hospital to make his rounds and very conveniently for Mother, left me at the Methodist Cradle Roll Sunday School across the street. If he was not finished by the time Sunday school was over, he sent a nurse to get me. We would sit outside on the edge of the fish pond in front of the hospital to wait for him. If it rained, the nurse took me to the basement to see the guinea pigs. I hope I did not pet any, since they were used as research in the laboratory.

After we got home on Sundays, Doc would hold me in his lap

while we read the Sunday funny papers together. When the days were long enough, he went fishing in the late afternoon. He kept a canoe, tied it to the roof of his car, and took it to the bayou, then paddled along, casting for bream, perch, or trout. The fish were almost dead by the time he got home, but I tried to revive them in the bathtub.

Doc's tackle box was almost as fascinating as his black doctor's bag. I really didn't like the doctor's bag at all. I can still smell the odor of the pinkish-red medicine he used to paint my throat. He would say, "Open wide," and stick the wooden stick coated with cotton down my throat. I can almost smell the odor now and feel the stinging sensation as the medicine coated my throat. He would then pat my hand and say, "Good girl."

My Surrogate Grandmother
by Sammye Munson

We called her "Mamie," my great aunt, who lived across the street from us. She was, in essence, my grandmother. All my grandparents died long before I was born, but Mamie and another great aunt, Aunt Annie, were surrogate grandmothers and gave me the love and attention I might have missed.

When I was in first grade, I walked to school and back. On this block-long walk, I passed Mamie's house, the yard blooming with red, yellow, and purple dahlias. Then I saw Mamie, her black curly hair and smiling face welcoming me from the porch of the house built in 1910.

Sammye Munson

"Hello, little darlin'" she'd say. "Have a good day at school?"

I usually said yes whether or not I had or hadn't. I wanted to see Mamie smile. She always had fresh ginger cookies baked in her ancient stove and cold milk delivered by the milkman that morning.

After I stuffed myself, we'd talk a bit before I headed across the street to my home.

Mother would greet me, but she didn't seem as

glad to see me as Mamie was. This routine occurred every day and lasted the school year.

My mother reminded me as I got older how Mamie saved my life. This sounded strange and unbelievable, but I wanted to believe it and still do. It has a magical ring to it.

This lifesaving act of Mamie's occurred when I was just a toddler, probably three or four years old. I caught the dreaded whooping cough (no vaccines in the 1930s) and coughed each time I tried to swallow food. Soon I refused to eat. I'm sure my parents were worried, even scared, for I was losing weight and no matter how much they insisted, I refused to eat.

Mamie was keeping me one day while Mother was gone. I was sitting at her small table in her kitchen. She coaxed me to eat, but I shook my head and clenched my teeth.

"Come, eat a little for Mamie," she'd say. "It's good."

She dipped a piece of bread in chicken gravy and brought it

Emma (Mamie) Slaughter

48

to her lips, smacking them to let me know how good it was. Then she dipped another piece in gravy and held it to my lips.

"Try it, for Mamie," she said softly.

I loved Mamie and wanted so much to please her, but I started to gag. Then I closed my eyes and opened my mouth, while she put a spoonful of soggy bread on my tongue. I swished it around a few times, then swallowed it. To my surprise and Mamie's, I didn't cough or throw up.

"That's a good girl. You're going to get well now."

Somehow I believed her. As she gave me a hug and kiss, I felt the softness of her hair on my forehead. Mamie had said I would get well, and Mamie didn't tell stories.

Gradually, I began eating soft foods and small portions. Slowly, I regained my strength and weight.

To this day I believe that Mamie, my surrogate grandmother, saved my life, with love as well as actions.

Grandmother Sammye Munson with grandson Christopher Munson

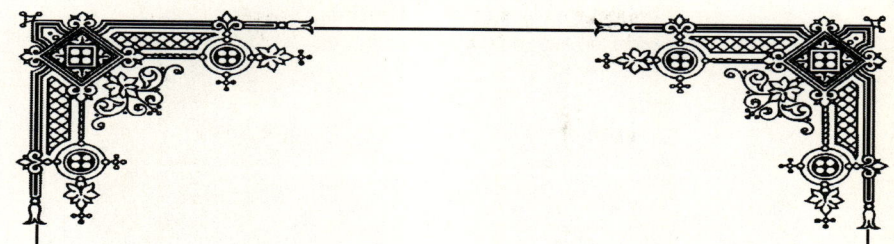

Faith and Love

You have read of the fun grandchildren have had with their grandparents. But grandparents also bequeath their grandchildren the gifts of faith and love. Spiritual ties are less obvious but still exist in this intergenerational relationship. A four-year-old can experience his grandmother's love that lasts for a lifetime in the writing of Mark Young. Generosity and compassion can also be learned from an elder, such as Sam Taub. N. Scott Momaday, the Native American writer, will never forget his grandmother's faith as she chanted her prayers.

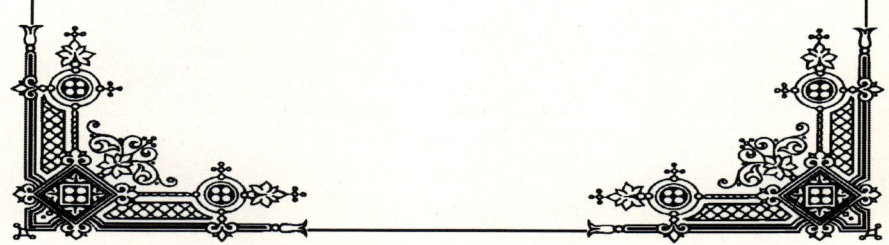

Mark Young and brother

The Goodbye Gift

by Mark Young

The leaves had not yet turned to shades of red and yellow. The Indian summer lingered as the Smoky Mountains bloomed their brilliance. It was farewell to summer and goodbye to Grandmother as we ended our vacation. It was also the closing days of a decade later termed "happy days." I was four years old in 1959.

As we packed up and said our farewells, there was joy in my grandmother's fifties face that brought familiarity and comfort to a young child. As I stood on tiptoe for that final embrace, I had no way of knowing that this was her goodbye gift.

She stooped down and combed my cotton top with her hands, telling me how important I was in this world. Her daughter, my mother, was expecting a new baby in a few months. It was my job to be a big brother and help take care of this little bundle, which would arrive in the fall.

As she hugged me, she said, "Take care, my little marathon: Grandmother will see you in a few months. Mind your mom and dad. And remember, always, that I love you."

Those were the last words I heard from Mary English Hartshorn. It was a true moment of innocence and permanence. Leaving the Blue Ridge Mountains of western North Carolina would never feel the same.

The memories of nearly forty years ago grow dim. But the recollection of Grandmother Hartshorn still holds fast because of her goodbye gift. Her words of love left me with a lifetime of gratitude. Words that would haunt me years later when I remembered the scene of my mother rocking my little brother in October of that year.

As Mother silently rocked, she also wept. As I knelt and looked up at her and my new brother, I didn't understand the tears. When

53

I asked, she said she was crying because she was happy. Later I learned that my grandmother had not come as she promised. She had died the day before my brother was born.

The doctors elected not to tell my mother about the death before my brother was born. They feared that the news could endanger my diabetic mother or her child. As I look back on that scene so long ago, I am reminded of the courage and compassion of my mother and grandmother.

"I give you a new commandment, that you love one another. Just as I have loved you, you should love one another." (John 13, 34).

Gifts have come and gone. Discarded, kept, lost, forgotten. But there is one gift I shall always remember. It will stay in my treasure chest from a time long past. I shall always treasure that gift and love you, Grandmother.

I Love You Best

by Daisy Akin

"Who do you love best?" I asked my grandmother.

"You, darlin'," she said, patting my hand.

"Mama," my mother would say, shaking her head, "you shouldn't tell Daisy that."

I smiled smugly but deep down I wondered if she did. It seemed to me that she loved all of her eight grandchildren intently. Yet she lived with me and my mother so I felt I had an edge over my cousins. Still, I knew I wasn't as wonderful as she thought I was.

My mother set high standards for herself and for me. She allowed me to have a great deal of freedom in my behavior and never interfered with the consequences that might follow. Baboo, my grandmother, was different. She always wanted me to be happy and to have what I wanted.

Daisy Brooks Akin

While Mother and Baboo didn't always agree on my upbringing, Mother usually prevailed and Baboo acquiesced. Sometimes Baboo would interfere if she thought that Mother was too severe.

One time, my friend across the street had a wonderful baby-doll that I admired and coveted. Peggy agreed to let me keep the doll overnight, even though Mother told me to return the doll im-

55

mediately. I kept the doll, and somehow, I broke its arm. The next morning Mother told me to take the doll back to Peggy and tell her what I had done.

I cried and carried on, begging Mother not to make me admit my clumsiness to my best friend. She stood her ground and told me that I had broken the doll and must bear the consequences.

After Mother went to work, I was crying and saw Baboo with a stricken look on her face. She hated for me to be unhappy. She didn't say anything to me but she made several phone calls. Then she told me to get the doll and come with her.

She had called a taxi that took us to town to a "doll hospital." The "doctor" fixed the arm as good as new while we waited. When we returned home, Baboo told me to take the doll to Peggy and not say anything, which I did. After Mother got home, she asked if I had returned the doll.

I said, "yes" with no further explanation This is only one of the many times my grandmother sweetened my life with her love and understanding. She's been dead over forty years, but not a day passes that I don't remember the scent of her cologne, her cool skin, and her gentle hands on my face.

Grandmother Daisy Brooks

56

Lesson in Kindness

by Mary Wright

Sam sat on the steps of the newspaper office shivering. It was winter in Texas and very cold at 4:30 in the morning. He got to the office early so he could get the papers first and be on the street before the other paper boys.

Sam, my grandfather, was only nine years old but had to help out by selling papers since the family had six children. He sold the morning paper each day before he went to school. Although he wore a warm sweater, the north wind blew right through him.

The family came to Texas when my grandfather was five. My great-grandfather left Hungary to find a better life and religious freedom. He crossed the ocean in 1876 in steerage, the lowest deck with bunks stacked on each other. He felt a new chance was worth the sacrifice.

Jacob, my great-grandfather, owned a pushcart and sold pots, pans, and ladies' trinkets to support his large family. Life was hard but as long as the family was together, they could survive. My grandfather said that his father once told him, "In this wonderful country, anything is possible."

Outside the newspaper office the young Sam shivered and pulled his sweater tighter. He hoped he wouldn't have to wait much longer. Suddenly, the front door opened and the editor, whom everyone called the Colonel, motioned for my grandfather to come inside. Sam hurried into the warm hallway.

"Come on, Sam, lie down on the couch in my office and get a little more sleep. I'll let you know when the papers are ready. It's too cold for you to wait outside."

Sam hurried into the warm hallway and managed a small smile. "Thank you, sir."

"The next time you're this early, just come on in and wait

where it's warm. Don't want our best salesman to catch a cold," the colonel added.

The years passed and the family prospered. Jacob, my great-grandfather, bought a wholesale tobacco business with the money he saved from his pushcart days. The oldest boys, my grandfather, and his brothers, Max and Otto, went into the business after they finished school.

Even Ben, the youngest, ran errands for his father after school. Many years later a hospital was named for him in Houston: Ben Taub Hospital. Otto decided to

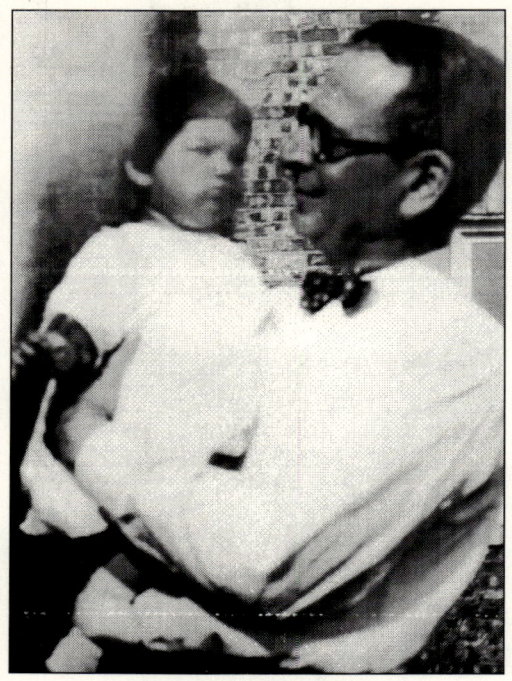

Grandfather Sam Taub with granddaughter Mary Wright

be a lawyer and attended the University of Texas Law School. The two girls married and started their own families.

My grandfather, Sam, was successful in the business. He never forgot the kindness of the colonel when he was a young paperboy. Years later he learned that the colonel's daughter was ill and destitute with no place to live. He arranged for her to live in a nursing home where she remained for the rest of her life. According to his wishes and in order to keep her pride and dignity, she never knew who her benefactor was.

My grandfather, Sam Taub, did many kind things for people in his lifetime. Yet this anonymous gift to an elderly, poor woman, impressed me the most. He never forgot the colonel's kindness when he was a poor paperboy.

Kindness is like a pebble thrown into the water. It creates many ripples as it reaches outward. I learned the lesson of kindness from my grandfather, Sam.

Mammy's Hands

by Stacey Hasbrook

Her hands, like a covey of quail, fluttered when she got excited. And sometimes as she remembered her Papa, they floated gently like an eagle gliding on sunlit air. For nearly thirty years I grew up listening to the stories of my great-grandmother, Mable Cox Shepard, born in 1894 to a pioneer family of Irish and English descent. She never truly cared for the name Mabel, so by the time I came to know her, she had already become "Mammy." Much of what I remember about her stories, of our wonderful years together, is the artistry of her hands.

As a child, I sat still for hours watching this fiercely independent woman earn a living as a seamstress. Her hands meticulously guided yards of material until a beautiful garment developed. She taught me the delicate task of threading a needle and how to make a dainty knot at the end of the threads, just so. And she taught me how to make small, careful stitches that didn't just service a seam but created an elegant finish. She completed the garment by hand with pride at the quality that a personal touch created, the same standard she applied to the daily agenda of her life.

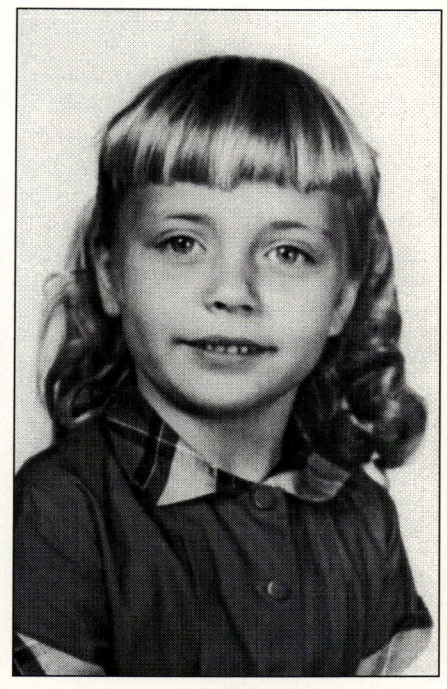

Stacey Carroll Hasbrook

Mable Cox Shepard
(Mammy)

Later her hands would ply magic out of a portable organ keyboard. A relative had found it second hand and gave it to her. With symphonic sounds she took me back to the days of silent movies, and in the dreamy hazes of my mind I watched her play the musical background to those great originals we call the classics. She would lean her head to mine and whisper that such a profession was not acceptable for a young lady of genteel persuasion. The sparkle in her eyes and smile let me know how she loved the drama her breach from polite society made. The images of her hands dancing on the keyboard in a darkened theatre ran through my sleep at night.

The final lesson Mammy's hands presented forced me to face life as an adult. During my sophomore year at college, when I was twenty, my aunt, her granddaughter, died from cancer. Since Mammy had survived a bout of heart trouble, she could not travel to the funeral in Houston. The family entrusted me to stay and care for her in her grieving. I quaked at the weight of responsibility. I cried alone with fear that I was too weak to hold back Death should He come to her door.

For three days we suffered together as she taught me the grace of loss. Sitting straight, head high, she gently rocked away the hours talking of "her angel gone before her." She reminisced about wonderful times and celebrated the glory of someday meeting her again. As she spoke, she absently stroked a delicate white handkerchief edged with handmade lace, raising it only to dab her eyes. Periodically, she patted my hand.

When the time came for me to return to school, she gently placed my palms together and enveloped my hands in hers with a quick, silent prayer. Then she cupped my face with those expressive hands, looked at me, and whispered, "I'll always love you."

To this day I close my eyes and can remember before I fall asleep the gentleness of her hands and the faint whiff of rosewater and glycerin.

Weather Eye
by Jean H. Marvin

Jean H. Marvin

My grandmother was raised
in the thunder-loud farmlands
of Arkansas, knew tornados
in green air that picked up barns.

Whenever the day sky darkened
and lightning fired in a rising wind,
she called her children in from play
to crowd under the feather bed.

Even now my mother remembers
the dusty smell of the feathers,
the flinch and the crash
of the cruel white light.

*On opposite page: Grandmother
Lillie Kelley*

62

Grandmother Lillie Kelley

by Jean H. Marvin

My grandmother's pleated
   cheek felt
soft as talcum, pressed
   against mine.
The strong brush strokes
   of her eyebrows
were dark as her ink black
   hair
streaked white, pinned up.
The love of a joke showed
   in her smile
and a long patience in her
   eyes.

Grandfather and the Child

by Dr. David Watts

Grandfather and the child
life's horizons
side by side
sharing secrets together
with laughter
a bond unspoken
yet binding
a kinship intangible
yet so real
few words need fall
only smiles
and frowns
gestures and glances
a soft communion scintillating
with gentle mischief
playing games
on life
spoofing
with respect
sparring
with love
through each richness
the younger grows wiser
and the wiser, younger
the magic is
that both may grow.

I Have Her in Memory

from *The Way to Rainy Mountain*

by N. Scott Momaday

Now that I can have her only in memory, I see my grandmother in the several postures that were peculiar to her: standing at the wood stove on winter morning and turning meat in a great iron skillet; sitting at the south window, bent above her beadwork, and afterwards, when her vision failed, looking down for a long time into the fold of her hands: going out upon a cane, very slowly as she did when the weight of age came upon her; praying. I remember her most often at prayer. She made long, rambling prayers out of suffering and hope, having seen many things. I was never sure that I had the right to hear, so exclusive were they of all mere custom and company. The last time I saw her she prayed standing by the side of her bed at night, naked to the waist, the light of a kerosene lamp moving upon her dark skin. Her long, black hair, always drawn and braided in the day, lay upon her shoulders and against her breasts like a shawl. I do not speak Kiowa, and I never understood her prayers, but there was something inherently sad in the sound, some merest hesitation upon the syllables of sorrow. She began in a high and descending pitch, exhausting her breath to silence; then again and again—and always the same intensity of effort, of something that is, and is not, like urgency in the human voice. Transported so in the dancing light among the shadows of her room, she seemed beyond the reach of time. But that was illusion; I think I knew then that I should not see her again.

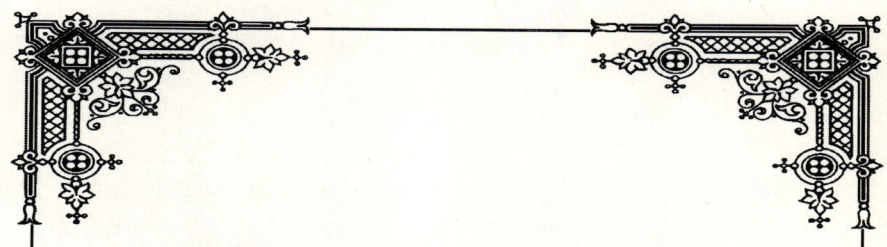

Gifts and Favors

The most meaningful gifts from grandparents are free. They are the gifts of love and time. They are special because they have no strings attached. For instance, Nana came to the school play and beamed as her grandchild performed, declaring with all sincerity that her grandchild was undoubtedly the best one in the production.

Papa was on hand the day his grandson fell and skinned his knee. He wrapped his long arms around the boy and brushed away the tears.

Another special gift was from Bubbie who spent hours sewing sequins on a ballerina dress for her granddaughter to wear in a dance recital.

Gifts from grandparents cannot be measured in dollars and cents. They involve the sensitivity of an elder who knows the value of a minute, an hour, and a word of praise.

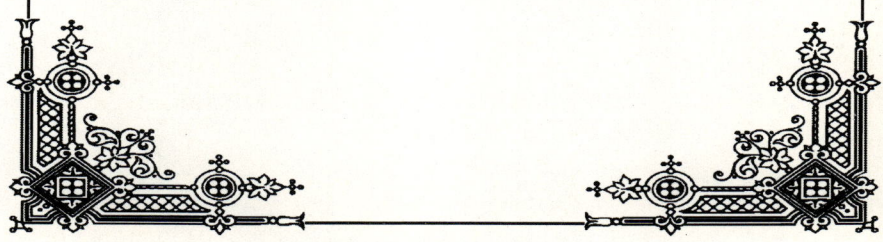

Papa

by Paul Munson

Papa, my grandfather, was a small, wiry man of Scotch-Irish descent. His frugality, whether from his Scotch ancestry or poverty as a child, matched his hatred of alcohol in any form. He was a tee-totaler and liquor never touched his lips, nor was there any in his home. He worked for Exxon all his life, saving everything he could, investing wisely, and at the end of his life had accumulated a size-able estate. He loved Exxon and for years after his retirement organized social affairs for annuitants. He was a people's person.

Papa never quite understood my acting career or why I wanted to pursue that life. He liked my high school plays and was proud of my acting, however. But the thought of my making a career in acting was incomprehensible to his practical nature.

I came home from California for a visit and naturally went to see Papa. I had been successful making commercials and was able to support myself, which pleased him. Still, he was dubious. He quizzed me about how much I earned for commercials. I took out a check stub from my pocket and tried to explain.

"I earn $100 each time the commercial plays on television," I told him.

His mind did some quick arithmetic as I mentioned the number of times the commercial was seen. It amounted to quite a nice sum of money. Papa's eyes lit up as he calculated the sum I had recently earned on one commercial.

"That sounds fine, my boy. What are you advertising in the commercial?"

I hesitated, wondering whether to tell him the truth.

"Well, what are you advertising, Paul?"

"It's a beer commercial, Papa."

Pause.

He looked down at the floor, then at me. A longer pause. He stared at the check stub. "Well, Paul, some things just can't

68

be helped. You gotta do what you gotta do," he said, with a wink and a smile.

Paul Munson with grandfathers
Joe Munson and Sam McLelland

Tatting for a Bike

by Mary Jane Sinclair

Ba-ba, my grandmother, was born at the end of the nineteenth century. She lived through two world wars, the Great Depression, and other traumatic events that shook the world. She also survived my brother's and my shenanigans. When I was born, she was sixty years old but had the energy of a woman half her age, my mother said. She firmly believed that nothing was impossible if a person sets her mind to it.

When my mother returned to work, I was fifteen months old and had the good fortune to spend my days with Ba-ba who lived just four blocks from us. Ba-ba and I had the greatest of times. One of our favorite things to do was to take the city bus to downtown Houston. We visited Ba-ba's favorite stores, Kress and Woolworth's. We browsed among the variety stores' many offerings and at the end of the morning, my grandmother treated me to lunch at the Kress lunch counter. I thought it was the grandest of restaurants. Our frequent trips aboard the "shoppers special" seemed to me, as a preschooler, like a trip around the world.

Fairy Jane Hughes, Grandmother "Ba-Ba"

One day in Kress's department store, I saw a kelly green bicycle. "Will you lift me on the seat?" I asked my grandmother. She did this, then stepped back to see me astride the bicycle in the middle of the main aisle of the store. I must have looked ecstatic for she asked me if I thought I was big enough to ride the bike. "Oh, yes," I said without hesitating.

She took note of the price tag then, lifted me off the bike, and we walked down the aisle to the store's exit. I couldn't get the bike out of my mind and mentioned it on the bus as we rode home. Ba-ba said nothing.

After a long day of doing household chores and keeping me, she often relaxed by doing her "handwork," tatting. Tatting is the lost art of lace-making. With a small metal shuttle that held a bobbin of thread, she made intricate webs of lace. She tatted baby booties and designs called "hens and chickens" used to trim pillowcases.

Over the next few months, I noticed her tatting more than usual. She fashioned booties, sets of pillowcases, and handkerchiefs. They did not stay long in the house but were picked up by friends. She worked feverishly, but the handwork disappeared as quickly as she finished it.

One day she said we would drive the car to town for a special reason. As we parked near Kress and got out, she then told me her surprise. She had sold her handwork to others and saved enough money to buy the kelly green bicycle. I couldn't believe that she had worked all those months with her nimble fingers to earn the money for my bike. She showed me the meaning of doing nice things for other people.

Mary Jane Sinclair

After her death, we found a small box in her top bureau drawer. As I opened it, I saw my name written in her handwriting on a piece of paper. Beneath the paper lay a pair of baby booties for her great grandchild not yet born. Eleven years later my daughter was born. I placed my grandmother's tatted booties gently around her tiny feet. My grandmother remains with me now and forever.

71

The Summer That Changed My Life

by JoAn Martin

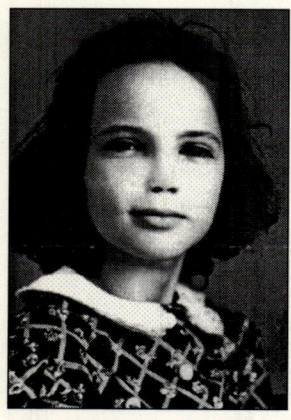

JoAn Martin

World War II was raging the summer I was eleven years old. Times were difficult for the hardware business that my parents owned. Since materials went to the war effort, it was hard to find anything to sell. My dad often traveled to Chicago or Pittsburgh, trying to buy goods to sell. My teenage brother was on the way to becoming a juvenile delinquent and my older sister was the beauty of the family. Where did that leave me?

"Go outside and play with your sister. Don't bother me. I'm busy," my mother said too often as she tried to handle the store's bookkeeping.

Then my Texas grandmother came to visit and invited me to ride the train home with her and stay awhile. I was thrilled to ride the train and have a new adventure but most of all to get away from the rejection I felt at home.

Big Daddy met us at the train station in Dallas with a smile on his face, delighted to see me and include me in his life. As a rural mail carrier, he rose early each morning, drove to the post office, and sorted cards, letters, and packages. With the mail stacked in order, he'd return to the house for me.

I loved driving those country roads with my grandfather, seeing the rich black dirt on the farms. The cotton and corn were head high as we drove in Big Daddy's Nash Rambler, his pride and joy. "Not a car in the country as good as this one," he'd say.

As we came to each mailbox, he'd tell me the occupant's name, and I'd slide the letter from the brown leather belt and hand him the mail for each family. He was patient with me as I learned to do this simple job. We both rejoiced when we saw a V-Mail envelope, knowing it was from a son who was fighting overseas. He'd then tell me the life history of the family. He treated me with respect, knowing I'd understand his long-winded stories.

Sometimes the owners would be standing by their mailboxes with three pennies to buy a stamp or just waiting for a chance to socialize. Big Daddy proudly introduced me as his granddaughter from South Alabama, then told them he didn't know how he ran the route before I came to visit. The ladies often offered us cookies or a jar of cold buttermilk.

Big Daddy would drop me off at noon while he went to the post office to take the mail he'd collected. After we ate a fresh vegetable garden lunch (we called it dinner), I helped Big Mama wash dishes. Then she'd lie on the bed to rest and catch the breeze flowing through the windows. I brushed her long hair just before she took a nap.

One of the most exciting experiences was going to the pasture and finding a new baby calf. I'd help chase the cow and Big Daddy would claim I was the very best helper he'd ever had. For the first time in my life, I felt that everything I did and said was wonderful.

In the cool of the evening after we finished our chores, we'd sit on the porch that wrapped around the two-story white house. One day, as we sat in the swing, Big Daddy asked me about my home and family. I welcomed the chance to tell him my feelings. I told him that my mother was too busy for me, and he knew I felt unhappy and unwanted. He patted my hand and smiled. I knew I was important to him.

I gained new confidence in myself that summer, a confidence that carried over to my life with my parents. I was able to cope with family members without feeling so worthless. Perhaps my mother heard from her father that his favorite grandchild needed more love and attention. But more likely, my new-found confidence came from spending the summer with my grandparents, being the center of my grandfather's life, and enjoying the praise he handed out so freely and sincerely. I knew I was important.

Pioneer Grandmother

by Geneva Fulgham

Grandmother was an English pioneer,
set down on Texas's humid eastern shore
with half her dozen siblings, in a year
when lack of Southern cotton troubled sore
the English mills, and spread the damage more
of Civil War. She with her husband Ned
and baby chose to try new scenes instead.

Grandmother was a farm wife and a cook
and keeper of the kitchen garden, too.
To plant potatoes she would always look
for moonless nights; no other ones would do.
She made good butter, and she learned to woo
vexed hens to nest and stubborn geese to lay;
her animals knew whom they should obey.

Grandmother was afraid her only child,
too fanciful, might find it hard to earn
her way; the daughter, quick to learn and mild,
became a teacher and a wife. In turn
five children came. Her chief concern,
they brought her, widowed, home to stay for good
with Grandmother, herself in widowhood.
Grandmother was a thousand things to me
and, now she's taking tea with cherubim,
I know she's teaching them how they must be
decorous when they sing a stately hymn,
and glad to eat their blackeyed peas with vim.
Preparing angels for a Heavenly quiz
and scolding, soothing, my Grandmother is.

Popo and Shakespeare

by Jo Ann Roberts

The richest man I have ever known was my maternal grandfather, William Carroll Kellum. He left an estate of $4. One of the riches he left to me was his love of literature. My brother and I called him "Popo" and although he has been dead almost fifty years, he lives in my memory.

Popo was born in 1869 during the Horatio Alger age, after the Civil War, when Southerners had little money and sketchy educations. Popo said there were three books that all families carried with them no matter how far they traveled: the Bible, Shakespeare, and *Pilgrim's Progress*.

Orphaned at an early age, Popo was fearless and adventuresome. At age eighteen, he had traveled from Kansas to Colorado to the Yukon on a surveying team. Traveling on horseback and on sailing ships, he endured real dangers. The love of his life was poetry and prose, which must have sustained him on those perilous and lonely trips.

Much later, after my grandmother died, Popo visited each of his four children for several months at a time. It was always an exciting event when he came to see us. Senor Dickey, as Popo called my brother, and I knew good times were coming. I wonder today just where Popo got the money to treat us every day to the "cream man," or to the local cafe where we ordered Fritoes and Delaware Punch.

Each evening Popo told us a story: *Ali Baba and the Forty Thieves, Robinson Crusoe* and Friday, and of course, all Bible stories. He also recited Southern folk poetry.

But Shakespeare was the real stuff. No watered-down version, but word for word. Popo's favorite was *Hamlet*, then *The Merchant of Venice*. He wove a fairyland of wonderful adventures where nothing terrible happened and the good guys won. My brother and I felt we were the good guys and we could win, too. Besides the fun,

Popo also gave us a love of good literature. I attribute my love of books and reading to the many nights we sat near him and listened to his enchanting stories.

Jo Ann Roberts

From Faraway Lands

Many grandparents lived or still live in other countries. We appreciate their culture, language, and traditions, which make our lives and country richer. Some of us are fortunate to hear stories about growing up in another country from the lips of our grandparents while others must rely on oral histories from other family members. We celebrate our own and others' differences.

Afternoons with Mormor

by Mary Jane Anderson Hopkins

She occupied the corner room at the back of the big house, the room wrapped around by windows from which we could see the gnarled old mulberry tree. In the summer, when the berries ripened, my brother and I filled our pails with berries and proudly offered them to Mormor (Grandmother in Swedish). She would clap her hands with delight.

"Tack så mycket," she said in lilting Swedish.

Grandma Anderson, whose given name was Emma Youngquist, lived with us on the farm when I was a girl. I was filled with wonder and a sense of excitement as she told stories of leaving her country and family at age sixteen to travel by ship to America. There she married and bore ten children in the big house built for her by my grandfather. She never returned to her native land but eagerly scanned the *Texas Posten*, the weekly Swedish newspaper, for news of her homeland.

Grandma's stories were sometimes funny, sometimes sad. She told these stories in the afternoon at about four o'clock, the traditional coffee time for Swedish people. As children, we could never invade Grandma's privacy during the day unless we were invited. But at coffee time, it was different. This was our time, to sip coffee milk, eat thin, crispy sugar cookies, and listen to her stories.

"One Sunday," she began, "as I hurried to get all ten children ready for Sunday school, your grandfather came to me, holding his starched white Sunday shirt in his hand."

"Emma," he said, "this shirt is not ironed properly! Please do it over!"

At this, Grandma's clear blue eyes sparkled with mischief. She titled her head.

"And do you know what I said then?" she asked.

"What, Mormor"? we said in unison.

"I took that shirt and dumped it in a pail of water and said, 'Oscar, if you want that shirt ironed, do it yourself.'"

We laughed and laughed.

At Christmas time every year, I saw the sadness settle in Grandma's face. She told us the story of Maude, her little girl. It was Christmas Eve, 1900. It was traditional for friends and neighbors to gather at the farm for a bonfire to celebrate the season. Children played tag and hide-and-seek in the cool December air. That night, however, when Maude was two, a gust of wind blew the flames onto her long dress and enveloped her. She died that night.

Grandma wiped tears from her eyes. She could never forget that tragedy, and I have never forgotten the expression on her face and the tremble in her voice. I shared her grief. Still, Grandma could put this grief aside and be fun, too. In the evenings on the wide front porch that circled the house, we sat in wicker chairs and played Chinese Checkers. I was certain that Grandma was the best checker player in the world. To this day, I do not think she let us win on purpose.

And I still love to play Chinese Checkers!

Mary Jane Anderson Hopkins
(above)

Mamie Anderson (below)

I Remember Belfast

by John McGarvey

In April 1941, when I was four years old, I experienced my first real feelings of fear and love. I lived in Belfast, Northern Ireland, and the city had become a target for long-range German bomber aircraft. One Sunday night we had a particularly fierce air raid, and I remember my mother and father crying in fear, and, of course, sensing their terror, I cried in unison. I think I experienced real fear at that moment. My mother and father realized that the situation could get worse and sent me and my fourteen-year-old sister to stay at my paternal grandparents' house that was in a safer area on the edge of the city.

My parents had taken my sister and me to visit there regularly for lunch each Sunday. However, visiting one day was different than staying, and besides, I had never been happy in that strange

Hugh Howard McGarvey (left) and John McGarvey

place. My grandparents' home had no electricity but used coal gas lighting. Gas mantles have a peculiar hiss, at least they did in my grandparents' home, and the sound frightened me. In addition, Sunday lunch was always a very formal affair. We sat in the dining room with no conversation except "Would you please pass this or that." After lunch everyone retired to the parlor or sitting room where we sat in silence except for this hissing of the gas mantles. It seemed like a million years but probably was only half an hour. Eventually, my grandfather would announce that my sister could now play the piano and entertain us.

Life in Northern Ireland was very staid; the people there took Victorian values to the extreme. For example, the swings in the park were chained up on Sundays, lest anyone actually enjoy themselves.

There I was, in shock from the bombing plus being in this strange place with many unpleasant experiences, particularly having to be still and quiet. However, my greatest unhappiness was being separated from my mother and father for the first time. I don't remember my sister in this stage of my life as she floats in and out of my recollections. She provided no comfort to me, as far as I remember. So there I was, a frightened little four-year-old, completely out of my comfort zone.

My grandfather was a retired nurse and my grandmother was a semi-retired midwife. During World War II, my grandfather was a volunteer air warden. The second day I was there, my grandfather took me with him to the air-raid warden's center, which was a large country house close by. I had no voice in this; it was a "royal command." When we got to the post, I was surprised to see a room with a large table covered in green baize (a course felt-like fabric), with edges all round and colored balls on it.

"I'm going to teach you to play snooker," my grandfather declared. He proceeded to do so with great patience and love (and probably great trepidation as to what a four-year-old can do to a snooker table surface). Life turned around for me that day. And snooker and billiards are still natural to me.

Today there is no greater soothing sound to my ears than the hiss of a gas mantle. My mind streams back to the agony of those Sunday lunches and to the fear that vanished around a snooker table. But most of all, I remember the love my grandfather gave me that day and ever after.

Remembering Zaidie

by Mike Hecht

My grandfather immigrated to America from Russia in the early 1900s, settling in South Chicago. He ran a kosher butcher shop. Plucked chickens. Cut meat. Gave honest measure. Kept his thumb off the scale. All this, mind you, when he wasn't in the South Chicago Synagogue on Houston Street praying or studying.

My first memory of Zaidie was in 1923 at the Jewish People's Institute. He and my grandmother were celebrating their sixtieth wedding anniversary. I was four years old.

I can still picture him, standing proud and erect at 5 feet 6 inches. He wore a black yarmulke on his head. His eyes twinkled and he seemed to smile most of the time. About nine years later, at ninety-two, a widower and retired, he moved in with with his son, my Uncle Max, and my aunt. I was twelve, a freshman at Roosevelt High School.

By this time, I had come to know my Zaidie and I respected him. He was cheerful, always had a smile, a quip, a greeting. He always greeted me with a hug or kiss. I think I loved him even more than I loved my parents. If he had told me to walk on water, I would have tried to do it.

In May of that year I made my Bar Mitzvah. The Monday after, Zaidie came to my home saying that since I was now a man in the Judaic sense, I needed to behave like one. Before going to school, I must put on my prayer shawl and pray.

Despite my adolescent ignorance, I knew Zaidie would not live forever. I also understood that I was Zaidie's last hope, the hope I would carry on the Judaic tradition as it had come down to him from Abraham, Isaac, and Jacob, then pass it down to my children. Without argument or protest from me, we sat down at the dining room table and began to pray.

That afternoon when I got home from school, eager to change

clothes and go outside to play ball, Zaidie was sitting at the dining room table, prayer book in hand. From May 1932 to June 1935, when I graduated from Roosevelt High School, we prayed six mornings a week at 7:00 A.M. and six afternoons a week when I got home from school.

Whether the Chicago weather was 95 degrees in the broiling sun of summer or 20 degrees below zero in winter, Zaidie would come, walking with his cane two miles to and from my home each day. In spring and during summer vacation, fall and winter, Zaidie would be at my dining room table, prayer book in hand. I was not exempt during baseball season. As my sixteen teammates waited for me, I felt the fever of bat and ball and bases run through my blood. And I began to race through my prayers to finish quickly.

I can still see Zaidie, sitting on my right side, his left hand palm face down across the page, right hand on my forearm, saying in Yiddish, "Don't rush, Mike. The ball game won't run away from you. Chant it, chant it."

And slow down I would, and chant it, I did. And at times when I was in good voice and making like a cantor, he'd be so taken with my chanting, he would pick up my right hand, bring it to his lips, and kiss my fingers.

Are there any, have there been any lover's kisses sweeter than Zaidie's on my fingers?

He died that summer of 1935 at age ninety-five, a few months after my sixteenth birthday.

Mah tow, ohalechaw Yacov, mishcanoasechaw Yisrael.

Mike Hecht, age 13, at his Bar Mitzvah, 1932

83

To Sweden with Love

by *Jean Sellstrom*

*Grandmother
Lena Gustafson Quist*

Grandmother Quist's yard was always filled with beautiful flowers, a vegetable garden, and nearby flowering fruit trees. She grew grass onions (like chives) that she snipped and sprinkled over her good, buttered homemade bread at coffee time. She had little money but when her grandchildren visited, gave each of us a few pennies from change she kept in a sugar bowl in her china cabinet.

Grandmother Quist was born Karolena Vilhelmina Gustafson in Sweden in 1868 and came to America in 1885 with the help of her older brother. On Sunday afternoons we would find her reading her Swedish Bible. She was not always able to get to church but she always read her scriptures.

She had not planned to remain in the United States but always planned to return to her beloved homeland. She saved her money working as an immigrant, hoping to save enough to return to Sweden. Then she met Grandfather Quist and married him. She was never able to return to her mother country. She consoled herself by saying that Sweden had probably changed so much that she would not even recognize it. In 1943 Grandmother Quist became an American citizen.

She spoke of Sweden in loving terms, telling us what a special place it was. I would try to visualize it as she spoke. I silently promised myself that I would someday make the trip to Sweden for her. She died in 1959, and in 1968, the year she would have been 100 years old, our family made our first trip to Sweden in her honor.

Grandmother Quist would have been proud that I learned Swedish and even helped translate the *Swedes in Texas* book. Maybe she was watching over me.

In 1994 my daughter and granddaughter, Liz and Rebecca Cadwallader, and I made another visit to Sweden. We were determined to bring back soil to put on my grandmother's grave.

The following is an excerpt that appeared in the Swedish newspaper:

"Jean Sellstrom held a little plastic bag in her hand. Contents: a handful of soil, more valuable to her than a Dala horse or Orrefors crystal. The soil was from Rosenberg, where her grandmother's home was. She hugged the bag with its brown contents and took it back to Texas with her."

We sprinkled the Swedish soil over my grandmother's grave. My daughter, Liz said, "Grandmother Quist never could return to Sweden, but we brought a little of Sweden back to her."

Jean Sellstrom, left, with Rebecca and Liz Cadwallader in Sweden

Dedecek's Missing Thumb

by Ursula Price

Faded family photos show grandfather without his thumb. Grandfather's missing thumb had been a family mystery for nearly a century. Josef Kalina emigrated to Texas in 1887 from Pisek, a village south of Prague in the Czech Republic. My siblings and I did not call him grandfather; he was and today remains in our memories as "Dedecek," Czech for grandfather.

Dedecek settled in the rolling hills of southern Fayette County in Praha, Texas, and carved out a living on his small farm. His passion in life was woodworking. When the field work was done, he would retreat to the nearby woods to carefully select and cut the oak tree that would yield wood for his woodworking projects. Not just any project, though. Money was scarce and household furnishings sparse. Dedecek used his talent to make furniture, kitchen cutlery, and utensils. The oaks would lend themselves to rolling pins, dough sticks, and chairs with benches of intricate-cut designs. Each was a gift from the heart for my grandmother, Maria, to commemorate special events in their lives.

Recently, I discovered my grandfather's journal and an entry on page 132 solved the mystery of the missing thumb. Little did I know that the story is linked to the rocking chair in my living room. The rocking chair is unlike others. It is rugged, plain, made of solid oak, strong and sturdy. It rocks with extreme ease and quiet, the way a rocking chair should rock.

On April 29, 1909, the ax missed its mark and Dedecek wrote in his journal, "roku 1909, 29 dubna sem is usekel palec." (in the year 1909, 29 April I cut off my thumb).

A year and some months later Maria received a rocking chair from Dedecek commemorating the birth of their son, Alois. The rugged and simple rocking chair that cost Dedecek his thumb now sits in my living room and was Dedecek's gift to my grandmother in honor of my father's birth.

Today the rocking chair opens itself as the pages of a book. It takes on new meaning and appreciation. I sit down and as I rock, I think of Dedecek. Patience, perseverance, peace, unconditional love, kindness—his legacy lives on in the gifts he made for Maria.

Dedecek's tradition of handmade gifts continues in our family. January 1 of each year marks our annual family reunion. Everyone has a gift for the person whose name they picked from the giftbox the previous year. Why do we select names a year in advance? We try to emulate Dedecek's gift-giving tradition with gifts that are handmade from our present resources. A year's advance gives us time to make this gift. Our Czech experience continues year after year as we share with each other jars of homemade jellies or jams, cutlery, embroidered linens or aprons, quilts, book racks, picture frames, wooden clocks, and chairs. We are carrying on Dedecek's, my grandfather's tradition.

Josef Kalina,
grandfather of Ursula Price

My Taiwanese Grandmother

by Mona Yu

I can visualize Po Po, my grandmother in Taiwan, remembering time spent with her when I was very young. She wore the traditional dress of an older Chinese woman, an indigo blue top trimmed in black with black pants. Her hair was pulled back in a small bun adorned with a white flower from the olive tree. I always knew when she was coming into the room by the scent of the olive flower. Her face was weathered by years of working in the sun growing rice in the rice paddies near her house. She worked hard all her life.

My sister and I were allowed to play in the rice paddies nearby. Rice plants are tall with sharp spikes, hazardous to touch. We often got scratched by the plants and ran into the house in tears. Po Po always knew what to do to soothe our irritated skin and calm us. I remember sleeping with her, as a child, and smelling the scent of herbs.

Po Po was an excellent cook and besides rice, she made a turkey dish for us with garlic and basil. Turkey was not available to buy in stores but Po Po raised chickens and turkeys. She lived, as many people in rural Taiwan did in the 1960s, in a family compound in the country. Her house was one of many owned by family members. There was no door in front of the house, only a curtain in the opening. We were all family in the compound and took care of each other. The back of the houses opened into a courtyard.

Mona Yu (right) holding sister Audrey

This country life no longer exists in

Mona Yu, left, with sister

Taiwan. Family compounds and rice paddies were destroyed to make way for industrialization. Because of this, I treasure memories of visiting Po Po. These early experiences with a caring grandmother will never be forgotten. They live in my heart.

Today I have a sweet olive tree in my Texas back yard to remind me of my grandmother and Taiwan.

Leslie Munson with grandson Matthew Munson

What Is a Grandparent?

A grandparent lets you watch television after bedtime at his house.

A grandparent puts a cold towel on your head and doesn't leave even when you throw up.

A grandparent frames the first picture you drew in first grade and puts it on the refrigerator.

A grandparent comes to your beginning band concert and claps and claps even if the band is out of tune.

A grandparent comes to every ball game even though you don't get to play. A grandparent may ride hours on the bus to come see you.

A grandparent buys the birthday cake you want with purple icing.

A grandparent takes up for you when the bully of the block teases you.

A grandparent teaches you to play "Chopsticks" on the piano.

A grandparent lets you spend the night at his or her house any time you want and even sleep with him or her.

The special relationship between a grandchild and grandparent is one neither will ever forget. The time and love so freely given can sustain a child through many rocky times reminding him or her that a grandparent thought he or she was special.

Years and separation my occur but the bond formed early in life remains. If you doubt this, read the following paragraphs written by children in elementary school.

Most were in the second grade, some in fifth. The younger children are from St. John's School in Houston, Texas. The older ones are from the Katy Independent School District.

We thank the students, their teachers, and administrators in encouraging them.

Grandma Mary
by Gabriel

I love my Grandma Mary. She comes on the bus for 8 hours to visit us. She always brings my sister and me presents. She sends us cards and money on holidays and visits us on our birthdays. One time I went to visit my Grandma Mary in San Angelo. It is about 300 miles from Houston. We went outside and played tag, then we went in the house because it was getting dark. Then we ate dinner and went to bed. Grandma has diabetes. She never eats any sugar. Grandma mostly speaks Spanish. She says she is a Tejana. Her family has always lived in Texas, even when it was part of Mexico. Grandma is fun.

My Grandmother, Me Me
by Tyler

Grandparents are the best. Unfortunately, I only have a grandma. Still, we have a good time. Every Friday she babysits. We watch t.v., make tea and play Liverpool rummy. Also, at other times she buys me books, takes me to eat pizza and shopping. Instead of calling her "Grandma," I call her Me Me. It's French for Grandma. I think I have the best grandma ever.

Fun, Fun, Fun with Grandparents

by Lawson

My grandfather and grandmothr live in California. Their names are Granny and Gramps. Granny is in a wheelchair. She has gray hair and hazel eyes. I love her very much. Gramps has gray hair, too, and blue eyes. I love him very much. When they visit, we play Monopoly. Last time my little brother, Christopher, won. I wish my grandparents lived in Texas.

Lucky Me
by Garrett

My grandparents are really special. They take me to the beach and camping. They invite my family to celebrate all of the holidays. My grandparents take care of me when I'm sick when everyone else has to go to work.

My Grandpa Joe takes me fishing with my dad. My Grandma Billy takes me swimming with my cousin.

My Grandma Carel takes me fishing, swimming and lets me to to my friend's house next door. My Grandpa Jay takes me to a place where I can feed the fish.

MeeMaw and Me
by Elizabeth

MeeMaw and I always bake
something like pies or cookies.
She makes apple pie for me and
pumpkin pie for my cousin,
Kelly. We always bake a batch
of cookies for me to take home.
Now I told you before but I will
tell you again, MeeMaw and I
love to bake!

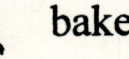 bake!

bake!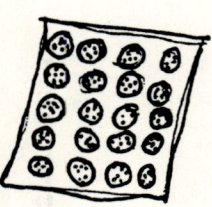

And I love her very much.

Special People
by Jada

My grandparents are very special to me but I don't see them very often. My grandparents and I keep in touch by writing to each other. I write my grandmother and she writes back. When school is out, for about two weeks, my grandparents come to get me. We drive six hours to get to Louisiana. Then it feels great to get out of the car. In the morning when we wake up, my grandmother makes me chocolate pop tarts and hot cocoa. We swim and have a lot of fun for two weeks. It's really cool when I go there.

My Grandparents   by Adam

I love my Papaw. At the ranch, we are always together. We are best pals. He lets me drive the "gator."

My Mamaw is beautiful and sweet. She likes golf and she likes to watch baseball. She takes me to Astros games.

Granddaddy and Bompa

by Hunter

I miss you, Granddaddy and Bompa. I loved you two and I wasn't ready for you to leave. I had no idea—you know what I mean. Hey! They wouldn't let me go to your funeral because I was so young. I'm doing o.k. in school. The question is for God. Are my grandfathers everywhere like people say they are, or just in our hearts? I'm taking Mom's advice. Please give me a nice, not scary sign. It doesn't have to be now, but maybe tomorrow or the next day. Please let me know because I miss my grandfathers. So does everyone. Why did you all leave? We all loved you.

God, I know now that they are everywhere.

Hunter and Granddaddy

99

Surprises and Memories
by Caroline

One hot summer day when the birds were chirping and a cool wind was blowing, Mama and Papa and I decided to pick the oranges on my grandparents' orange tree. There were so many and they were all ripe. I helped my grandparents put them in a big basket. I tasted an orange right after it was picked. It was really sour. My grandfather let me climb the tree in the yard. When he looks in my face, I feel good. I love my grandparents. They're always there when I need them.

My Grandmothers
by Clayton

Mamaw has lived with us since I was born and before. My grandmother Mamaw always will help me make cookies. Sometimes I go into her room to watch TV. Other times I play board games. Sometimes we watch movies. And she makes me turkey sandwiches for lunch every day. She knows just the way I like them. I love her.

My Grandmother Mutt likes to help me grow things like lima bean plants and crystals. She always keeps me company. We read books. Sometimes we play games. Other times we watch movies. Her favorite book is the Bible. My favorite movie is "Look Who's Talking."

Nanny and Grandpa

by Allison

My grandmother's name is Norren but I call her Nanny. She is a thoughtful person. She has gray hair. I don't know what color her eyes are. Some of my memories with her are making Play-do. I remember how that ooshy-gooshy stuff felt between my fingers. I accidentally ate some. It tasted good. I like to play at her computer. I typed a story, called "My Life." It was about me growing up. Nanny also has a closet full of toys. She measures how much I grow. She takes me to McDonald's. She always has a twinkle in her eyes. I love her. She never misses my birthday or a holiday. My grandpa's name is Leslie but we call him Grandpa. He is a good drawer. He never misses anything. He also has a twinkle in his eyes.

G.P. and Elaine

Every year during the Jewish holiday called Yom Kippur, we have lots of our family to G.P. and Elaine's house. We have a big dinner. Sometimes my brothers and I go to their house in Galveston. When G.P. is with us, he cooks the best shrimp for dinner! I love my grandparents!

by Sarah

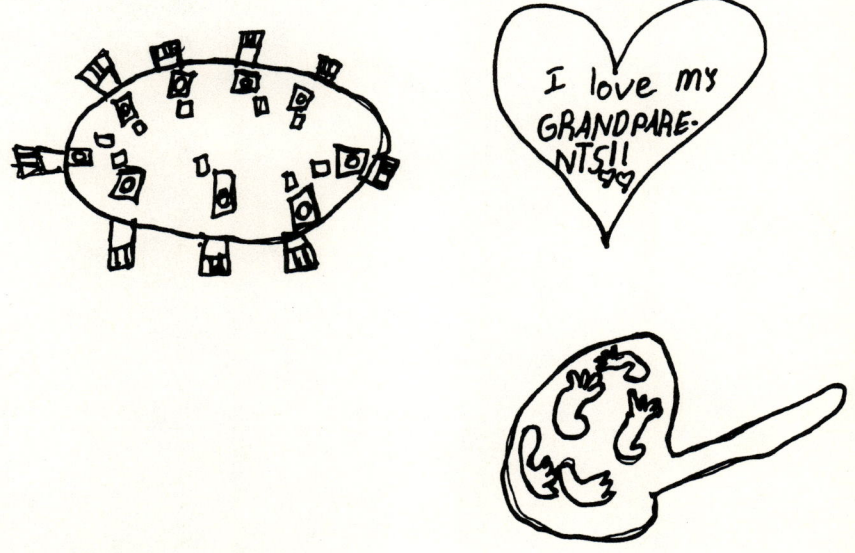

Missing Grandpa

by Ashley

    This is the first Grandparents' Day without my Grandpa. I miss him very much. I pray for him every night and it makes me sad to think about him. I wish he was still here. He must be happy where he is, but I still wish he was here with us. We used to go fishing together in his pond. The pond reminds me of him. He died when I was eight.

Grandparents

I love my grandparents so much! One time I went to Colorado and we had so much fun with them. I will always remember when we went skiing together. When I was little, my grandmother would get out balls and say, "What color is this?" Just a couple of days ago my grandfather put a game on the computer for me. I got my own icon. These are just a few of the reasons why I love them. They are nice and I will always love them!

by Mackie

105

My Grandmother

I Lae Mamie

by Grace

My Grandmother Mamie lives in Houston. I get to see her a lot. Sometimes she comes to our house for fun. She plays Scrabble with us. Sometimes I spend the night with Mamie on Saturday night. In the morning we go to church. One day we couldn't find my church classroom so we went back to Mamie's house and we made sheep out of cotton and said the psalm of The Lord Is My Shepherd. Then I went home.

My Grandparents
by Renee

My Grandparents live in New Mexico and in the city of Albuquerque. It takes a while to get from Albuquerque to Texas. I usually go to Albuquerque two to four times a year and we usually stay for the weekend. My Grandparents barely come to Texas. I really wish I lived closer. My Grandma has brown eyes. She wears glasses so she can read. Her hair is black. My Grandpa has white hair and a little hair on top and both sides. He wears glasses to read too. I really really love them and I really wish my sister Jacqueline and I could go to Albuquerque every Christmas. We had Christmas there long ago.

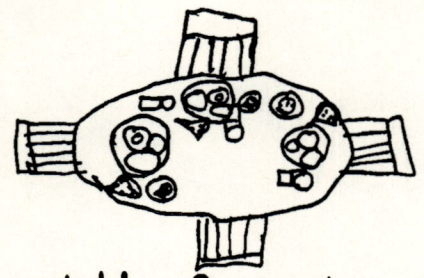

Me and My Grandparents

by Kirby

When I went to my grandparents' house last summer I got to stay there for two weeks. I like to go to my grandparents' house. We always go outside and pick okra and radishes. I know that my grandpa sits on a chair and tickles me in the stomach, and we both start to laugh. Every morning when I wake up there's a yummy smell of muffins and pancakes. I like to talk to my grandparents at the table, and when I'm finished with my breakfast I get to be a lazy head and watch TV. After I get dressed in my clothes, my grandmother brushes my hair and puts it in a ponytail. I want to go there next summer because it's so fun at their house.

Grandma and Me

by Ashley

My grandma lives with me. Once when my
grandma and I were at the Sharpstown Mall we
looked through Foley's. After that we walked all
the way to Luby's for lunch. I had fried chicken,
fried okra, corn and Jello. My grandma had roast
beef, fried okra and pecan pie. After lunch we
went to a cookie shop and I had an Icee. Then we
looked at toys and I got a purple gum ball from the
gumball machine. After that my mom came and
took us home. Anyway, I'm glad my grandma
lives with me because she is just like a second
mom.

Meme's House
by Rob

I like to go to Meme's house because she can cook very well. Almost every Saturday night my brother and I go to her house. My favorite foods that she fixes are cookies, cakes and pies. Sometimes she makes chicken nuggets. I also like to watch TV on her couch. She is very nice. She lives in Houston. She likes shopping, church, dogs, cats, birds and lots of other things. I like her a whole lot. She has curly hair and likes to wear dresses and shorts. She is a volunteer at Methodist Hospital. I think that's a really nice thing to do.

Grandparents in the Twenty-First Century

As the new century has dawned, we recognize changes in our society. Life in the twenty-first century is not a Norman Rockwell painting. Many grandchildren live far away from their grandparents, in other states or countries. Still, grandparents and grandchildren must stay in touch.

Bonds begin between grandparent and grandchild as soon as the child is born and continue to grow. I remember holding my preemie grandson a few hours after his birth, his fragile body warm against mine. I knew at that moment that I would love this child for the rest of my life. Nothing could dilute or banish this love. His life was the promise of the ongoing of our family.

Relationship problems with the child's parents can harm or destroy this intergenerational bond. Grandparents and grandchildren must try to keep the bond alive. Technology has made it easier. When the computer says, "You've got mail," the grandchild and grandparent smile.

Audios of a grandparent's voice can bring him into the child's world. Videos of children playing ball, playing in the band or at birthday parties can keep important occasions alive.

Summer vacations and spring or winter breaks offer opportunities for children to visit their grandparents. Elderhostels now offer vacations for both grandchild and grandparent. There are over sixty million grandparents in our country today, grandparents who are experiencing the joy of loving a grandchild.

About the Authors
(In order of their memories in book)

ALISON QUOYESER, former Texan, teaches in the San Francisco area.

LESLIE MUNSON, retired music educator in Houston, taught band and orchestra for thirty-five years.

MARY BELLE PATTERSON, former writer, editor, and research assistant, is now studying art.

TESS THOMAS is a freelance writer, computer buff, and active grandmother.

ANNA PEARL BARRETT retired recently as educator and has written several children's books, including *Juneteenth*.

GUADALUPE QUINTANILLA, a professor at the University of Houston, has done research on women writers and has written several books.

ESTELLE MOORE-WALKER recently won outstanding teacher of the year in the Houston Independent School District.

PAM ZOLLMAN, a freelance writer, writes and publishes children's books, stories, and poems.

BETTY DIENER, who grew up in Philadelphia, is a retired secretary in Texas.

DAN RATHER, anchor for CBS *Evening News*, was born and grew up in Texas.

LAURA BUSH, First Lady of the United States, former librarian and teacher, sponsors the Texas Book Festival.

CAROL BURNETT, actress, comedian, and author, spent her early years in San Antonio, Texas.

EUDORA WELTY, author of many books, is considered one of our country's outstanding writers.

JOAN NIXON, award-winning children's author, has published over 100 books and had her work produced on television. She is an active grandmother.

ANITA HIGMAN is the author of plays, books, and short stories, including *Tornado, Who Do You Want To Be For The Rest of Your Life*.

Carolyn Harrell Kilgore authored *When the Bells Tolled for Lincoln*.

Baker Akin is a retired businessman and grandfather.

Clayton Kellogg, former Texan, now lives in Monroe, Louisiana.

Sammye Munson is a retired teacher and author of five children's books.

Mark Young is a Methodist minister who enjoys writing.

Daisy Akin, an avid reader, lives in Bellaire, Texas, and is a grandmother.

Mary Wright is the author of *Stranded, Stormy's Adventures*. She also is a supporter of the Texas Marine Mammal Stranding Network.

Stacey Hasbrook is a freelance writer in Central Texas.

Jean H. Marvin is prolific poet and author of children's stories.

David Watts, a physician and poet in San Francisco, is a former Texan.

N. Scott Momaday, a Native American, writes about his heritage.

Paul Munson is the theatre arts teacher and director at Bellaire High School.

Mary Jane Sinclair, a professional harpist, is the author of *The Films of Leslie Howard* and lives in the Houston area.

JoAn Martin is a retired teacher and published writer in Baytown, Texas.

Geneva Fulgham is the author of mystery novels and an accomplished poet.

Jo Ann Roberts, a retired secretary, still loves books and reading because of her grandfather.

Mary Jane Anderson Hopkins is a published author, lives in Austin, and has eight grandchildren.

John McGarvey, a businessman, was born in Ireland and has the gift of words.

Mike Hecht is retired and lives in the Chicago area.

Jean Sellstrom is of Swedish descent, lives in Austin, Texas, and is a grandmother.

URSULA PRICE has written a cookbook celebrating her Czech heritage.

MONA YU is a pharmacist in a Houston hospital, working on her Ph.D. She was born in Taiwan and came to Texas as a graduate student.